THE
NEW
DAY

THE NEW DAY

EDITED BY
SAM RAGAN
RALEIGH, NORTH CAROLINA

PUBLISHED BY
RECORD PUBLISHING COMPANY
ZEBULON, NORTH CAROLINA

PRINTED 1964 BY
THEO. DAVIS SONS, PRINTING
ZEBULON, NORTH CAROLINA, U.S.A.

LIBRARY OF CONGRESS CATALOG CARD NUMBER 64-66239

TERRY SANFORD

North Carolina is facing a New Day.
 . . . the people of North Carolina are ready to go—ready to
make this New Day of opportunity a New Day
of achievement.

I want North Carolina to move into the mainstream of America.
 . . . I call on all citizens to join with me in the
audacious adventure of making North Carolina
all it can and ought to be.

Quality Education is the rock upon which I will build the house of my administration.

We must begin to swing the doors to the future for our children, for beyond the threshold lie the hopes and aspirations of not only our children but all the world's children....

The hour is at hand when North Carolina can begin its bold march forward. We begin this march in these halls by reaching out and grasping the hands of our priceless possession, our children and our grandchildren.

The hand we grasp today is the strong handclasp to the future, the hand of a leader in the world's struggles.

I thank you for your attention to the future of North Carolina.

—Budget Message on Education, 1961.

Governor Terry Sanford had just presented to the 1961 North Carolina General Assembly the first installment of his *"quality education"* program. He proposed to add $100 million to enrich the public school program.

A veteran legislator and longtime Sanford friend came to the Governor's high-ceilinged office in the State Capitol. With a knowing smile and in a confidential tone, the legislator said, "Now, Terry, I know what you have asked. But tell me, how much of it do you really want?"

"All of it," said Governor Sanford firmly.

He got the $100 million. And during the four years of his administration, the State made the greatest progress in education it had ever made in its long history.

The story could be told in terms of statistics, by reeling off columns of figures to illustrate the great increases in the amount of money spent at all levels of the educational process in North Carolina, by tabulating the number of new classrooms and other new buildings.

Betsy with her father in 1960.

Sanford preferred to tell the story in terms of people, even though he had to cope with the vexing problem of financing his ambitious, imaginative program. When he hammered away on the theme of improved education in the gubernatorial campaign, and later when it became the lodestar of his administration, he related it to the hopes and aspirations of boys and girls, the livelihood of unskilled adults, the trainability of the retarded, the demands of a technological age, and the role of citizens compelled to live and work in a rapidly changing, more complex world.

Sanford, the son of a school teacher, was imbued with the idea that education is the main artery of life itself. As he said, "There are direct correlations between the educational attainments of people and the crime rate. It costs less to educate the youth than it does to imprison and rehabilitate the adult criminal.

"There is a direct correlation between the earnings of a man and the number of years he spent in school—and what he learned during those years in school.

"There is a direct correlation in the investment a people make in education and the overall welfare of their community, state and nation. The best money a man spends to assure economic security for his children is the money he spends to educate them.

"There certainly is a correlation between education and human tolerance. Ignorance and intolerance are partners—just as are poverty and disease, and low income and low education."

Out-of-state businessmen, seeking sites for new plants, eventually posed the question to North Carolina: how good are your public schools and your universities and colleges? During the Sanford administration, they answered that question by investing a billion dollars within the State, another record for a four-year period.

While taking a native's pride in the "firsts" claimed by North Carolina in the South and Southeast, Sanford also said that these regional superlatives were not enough. North Carolina, he said, had the resources, human and natural, to lead the nation if the resources were properly developed. The State, he added, should quit gauging its progress against that of other

"If you have the will and skill, we will help you go to college." This was the promise of Governor Sanford to high school graduates in June of 1962. To make good on that promise, Governor Sanford worked with the North Carolina Bankers Association in setting up the Student Loan Program. That low-interest loan program is supported by the majority of the banks in North Carolina.

Governor Sanford, a graduate of the State University and chairman of church-related Methodist College, saw to it that private North Carolina colleges received assistance along with State-supported colleges under the Higher Educational Facilities Act. He also recommended tuition grants for students attending private colleges.

Always interested in a sound fiscal foundation, Democratic Nominee Sanford carefully studied the proposed budget recommendations which were to be his when he took office in January, 1961. His motto was "Fiscally Sound and Forward Bound" and the Sanford savings from appropriations were the largest in the State's history.

states in the region and use as a yardstick instead the most progressive states in the nation.

And what single thing could most effectively propel the State and its people into the mainstream of America, into a better life and a more secure future? Sanford's reply was *quality education.* He set out to do something about it.

In his campaign for the governorship in 1960, Sanford outlined his educational goals in great detail. With rare candor for a candidate seeking election at the hands of a tax-conscious electorate, he said that, if necessary, he would seek new tax sources to underwrite the program. Sanford's program, in essence, was that of the State Board of Education and the United Forces for Education, which embraces a number of interested statewide organizations.

As do all incoming Tar Heel chief executives, Gov. Sanford inherited the proposed state budget prepared by his predecessor and members of the Advisory Budget Commission. That budget for the 1961-63 biennium lacked some $70 million in funds Sanford and the educators considered essential to launch what the governor described as a long-range effort to upgrade the schools.

Next came the problem of finding the money. Sanford carefully sounded out individual legislators on their tax views. He considered and then rejected an increase in the 3 per cent sales tax. He eliminated a possible tax on soft drinks as being unfair, and a tax on tobacco products as being a political impossibility.

He finally settled on the extension of the sales tax to cover food items. It seemed a politically unwise choice. "Food tax" was a term admirably suited to sloganeering. Many legislators felt a vote for it would seal their doom (they were proved wrong). But Sanford pressed the point. Any tax, he said, is unpleasant. The great advantage to the food tax was that it would provide a continuing, growing source of revenue to meet the continuing, growing demands of the schools.

"Now that we're off the ground we can get rid of this balloon!"

> *If we tax bread, we also will be taxing cake; if we tax fatback, we also will tax caviar; if we tax corn meal, we also will tax filet mignon. . . .*
>
> *No one is going to go hungry because of this tax . . . But the children of North Carolina will go thirsty for quality education if we do not enact this program for better schools . . .*
>
> —From an address in Smithfield, N. C., March 9, 1961.

In looking back upon his administration, Sanford said that his most satisfying moment came the day the House enacted the food tax into law. At last, the money was available to give substance to the dream. This is what it purchased immediately:

—Pay increases for teachers and all other school personnel, including superintendents. Teacher pay raises averaged 22 per cent.

—Addition of 1,401 new teachers for 1961-62, 1,425 for 1962-63; addition of 44 assistant superintendents, 25 supervisors, and extra home economics and vocational teachers.

—Clerical assistance for schools, with $1.50 per pupil allocated to provide the clerks.

—Library allotment increased from 50 cents per pupil to $1, and instructional supplies raised from $1.12 to $1.50 per pupil.

—In-service courses for professional improvement of teachers provided at cost of $300,000, and 300 additional teacher education scholarships offered.

—Salaries increased for college personnel, and an additional $70,100 appropriated for expansion of television teaching.

—Increased funds for Industrial Education Centers, and a strengthened Department of Public Instruction.

—Established the Department of Curriculum and Research to keep curricula in the schools abreast of latest developments and techniques.

Because learning is an evolutionary process, many of the benefits of educational expenditures accrue, often almost im-

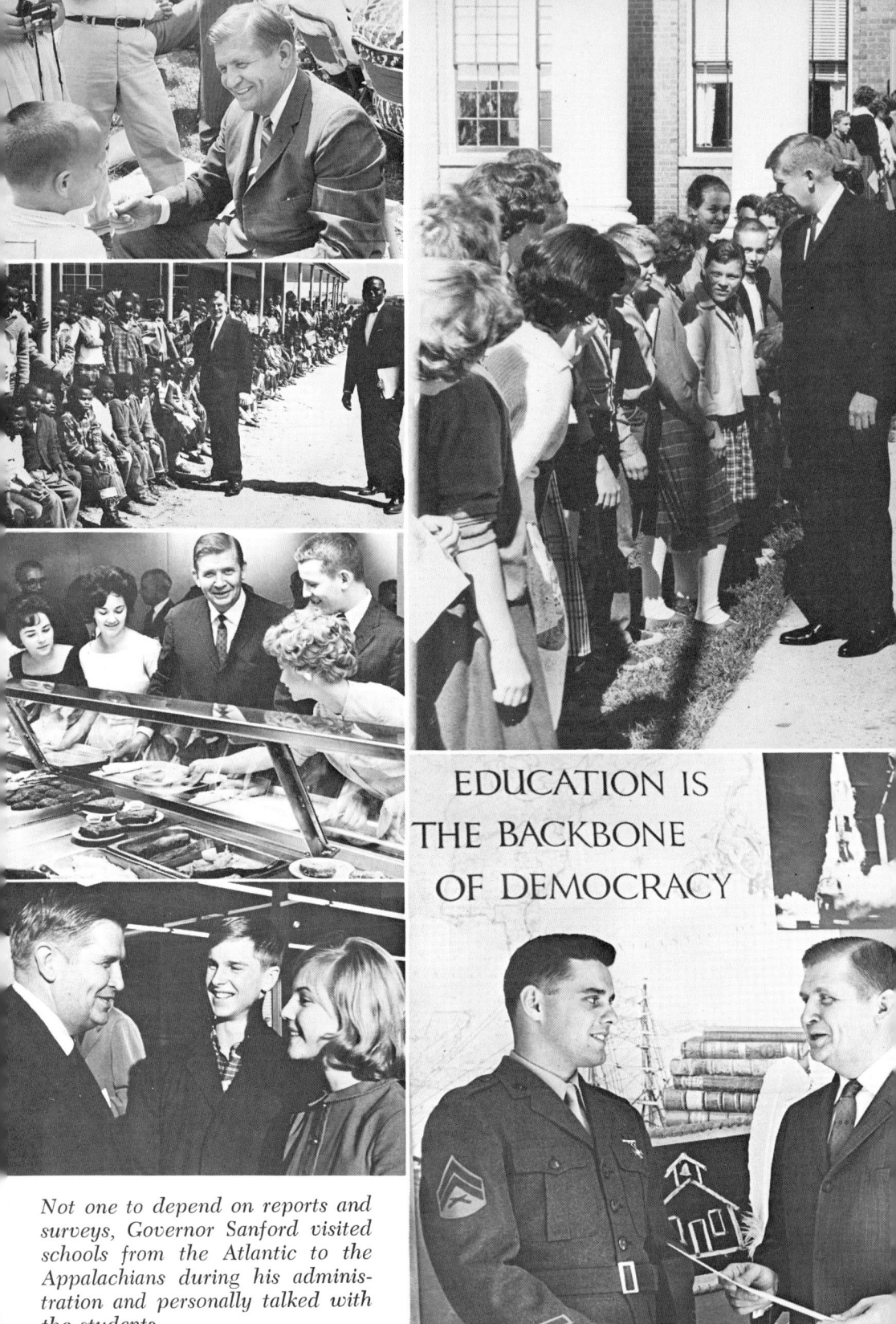

Not one to depend on reports and surveys, Governor Sanford visited schools from the Atlantic to the Appalachians during his administration and personally talked with the students.

EDUCATION IS THE BACKBONE OF DEMOCRACY

Governor Sanford went to the students with his television program on his program of Quality Education. Some 40,000 letters from school children of all ages poured into the Capitol. All were answered.

Mr. Cecil Sanford, Governor Sanford's father, is an independent merchant in Laurinburg. Below (right) Governor Sanford's daughter, Betsy, welcomes President Johnson's daughter, Lynda Bird, to the State in the spring of 1964.

perceptibly, over an extended period of time. That holds true for some phases of the Sanford program. But at the conclusion of the 1961-62 school year, national educational organizations said that North Carolina's rate of advance in support of the schools had been greater than that of any other state.

Also, at the close of 1961, the Department of Curriculum and Research surveyed local school superintendents as to the results of action taken by the 1961 General Assembly, composed, Sanford said, of legislators "of vision and courage." The superintendents noted a quickening of pace in the schools.

They reported improvement in the effort, interest and attitude of teachers, including improvement in the quality of applicants for teaching positions. Class size was reduced. Libraries were improved. More guidance services were provided, and more teachers assigned to special education classes. Students seemed more serious. Communities began exhibiting a more cooperative attitude, especially in the matter of eliminating interruptions of school time.

Nor was Sanford content to rest on these accomplishments. Having secured legislative approval of the program, he now embarked on a unique and unprecedented tour all over the State to speak personally to thousands of elementary and high school students. He told the students, in effect: the General Asesmbly has provided the tools, now it is up to you to use them wisely and conscientiously.

Veteran reporters, who attended some of these meetings (on some days Sanford spoke in as many as 15 different schools in several different counties), were impressed by the manner in which Sanford and the students, white and Negro, seemed to establish a close rapport.

In folksy language, he told the students how the world had changed ("There was no television when I was a boy, and the only space ships were operated by Buck Rogers in the comic strips.") and was changing. You need skills to get jobs, he told them, so you must study hard and learn all that you can. The students obviously were impressed that the State's No. 1 citizen would take time from his crammed schedule to visit them. Their letters of appreciation, many of them in childish scrawls, filled more than a score of big cardboard boxes in the attic of the State Capitol.

Mrs. Cecil Sanford of Laurinburg, Governor Sanford's mother, taught school for more than 40 years.

One girl in a grammar grade, who obviously had just discovered boys, wrote, "I think this quality education is fine. In my class there are five girls and 12 boys." A boy wrote, "When I grow up, I want to be an astronaut. If I can't be an astronaut, I will be Governor."

Sanford told a story to each group of youngsters. He said that at one school, after he had finished listing the discoveries and inventions which had not been made when he was in school, a child said, "Governor, did you ever meet President Lincoln?" When the youngsters laughed, Sanford added, "I'm glad you laughed. At the last school, they didn't."

> *We need a school system concerned with all hopes, all needs, all abilities...*
>
> *We need teachers who will hold out their hands of understanding to the slow and who will raise high the goals for the bright.*

The 1963 General Assembly was historic in setting and in accomplishment. It met for the first time in the new $6 million State Legislative Building designed by Edward Durell Stone. And, under the guidance of Gov. Sanford, it established some national precedents in the field of creative education, as well as charting a new course for higher education in North Carolina.

Not incidentally, to these main thrusts in higher education, Sanford prevailed upon the legislators to further enrich the public schools by appropriating approximately $52 million in new money beyond that required for normal growth during the 1963-65 biennium. Once again, Sanford made the program of the State Board of Education and the United Forces for Education his own and the General Assembly adopted it en toto.

The accomplishments for secondary education, although overshadowed by the giant steps taken in higher education, were considerable:

—Teachers were given a monthly salary increase of $15 for the first year of the biennium, $10 additional for the second, the pay of principals, supervisors and beginning teachers was raised.

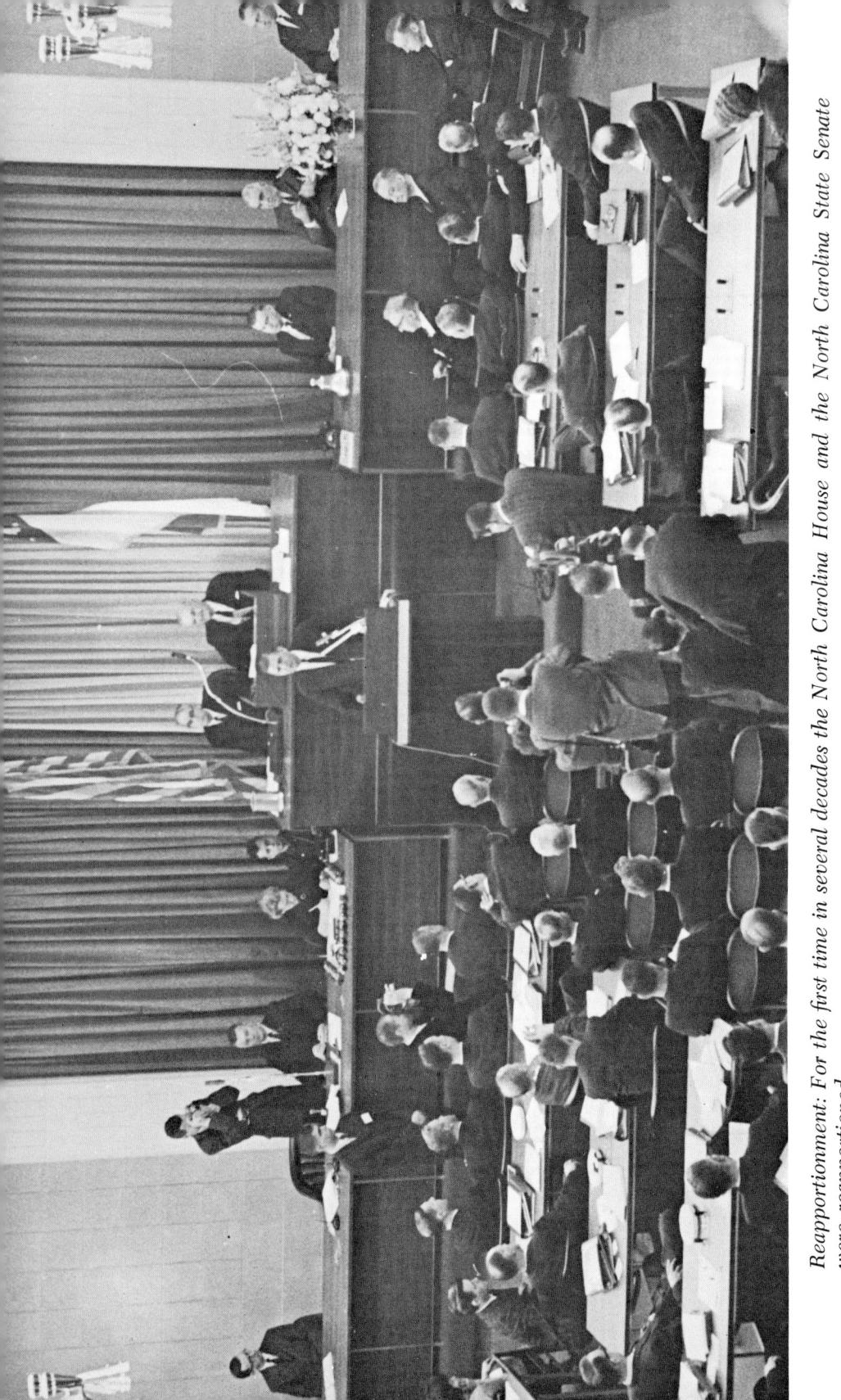

Reapportionment: For the first time in several decades the North Carolina House and the North Carolina State Senate were reapportioned.

—Teachers were provided five days of annual sick leave, cumulative indefinitely, and 450 additional scholarships for prospective teachers were authorized.

—Funds were appropriated at the rate of $4 per high school student for textbooks, and at the rate of 25 cents per pupil for film purchases and equipment for Industrial Education Centers.

—Forty-nine assistant superintendents and 65 attendance counselors were provided.

—Allotment formulas were altered to provide more teachers, reduce class size, provide librarians, guidance counselors and special teachers. Approximately 1,340 additional teachers provided.

—Three hundred special education teachers were authorized, 331 more teachers were provided for exceptionally talented children, and 630 new teachers were provided for vocational education.

In the four years of Gov. Sanford's administration, support of public education nearly doubled, up to $300 million a year.

In the reach for the stars, education provides the greatest power of thrust.

The Higher Education Act of 1963 ultimately may prove to be the most significant development in North Carolina since the State adopted the policy of universal education. It consisted of three main parts:

1. The Consolidated University of North Carolina was designated as the sole State university (to guard against the proliferation of inferior institutions) and given authority to expand to other campuses if the need can be shown and specified criteria met.

2. Machinery was established for the creation of a state-wide system of comprehensive community colleges, within the academic and financial reach of virtually anyone who wants to take courses ranging from auto mechanics to college parallel work.

As Chairman of the Board of Trustees of the Greater University Governor Sanford led the fight for expanding all branches of the University and of extending its educational mission.

Commencement addresses were standard engagements for the Governor every spring.

Mutual respect and assistance were the basis for the strong friendship between Governor Sanford and Lieutenant Governor Cloyd Philpott. Philpott's death in 1961 left North Carolina without a Lieutenant Governor and, many thought, deprived the State of a future Governor.

A father helps his son in Quality Education homework.

Often meetings extended far beyond the family bedtime . . . the clock seldom determined the length of important meetings.

3. Two-year community colleges in Charlotte, Wilmington and Asheville were converted, on a graduated basis, to four-year, state-supported senior institutions.

The Higher Education Act of 1963 provided for appropriations of $98 million, compared to the $56.3 million appropriated for the same purpose by the 1961 General Assembly.

The community colleges are attended entirely by commuters. There are no dormitories. It is estimated that a student taking college parallel work, which is accepted without hesitation by state-supported colleges and the university, can get by on $120 per year.

A unique feature of this system is the "open door" policy. Under it, an adult student, regardless of the level of prior attainment, may gain admission every time. No entrance tests bar the way to the freshman class, or to the technical institutes or Industrial Education Centers that are components of the comprehensive community college.

Students who demonstrate, in a series of examinations, that they are not prepared for the regular college work enter what is called the Fundamentals Learning Laboratory. This is an automated operation in which teaching machines and other new techniques, including individualized learning materials, are employed. A student proceeds at his own speed to accumulate the knowledge he needs to move to the college level.

A counselor supplants the teacher in this automated laboratory, administering the tests and guiding the student. There are no class sessions. Every student begins his studies the day he enrolls. By putting in a month of eight-hour days, he may complete a course that would require 180 days for the normal high school student. But a student who fails to make progress gets a failing mark.

The Industrial Education Centers offer high school juniors and seniors part-time instruction in varied trade and technical specialty courses, as well as adult education courses. Technical Institutes offer the same instruction, but add to the curriculum an organized program for the training of technicians.

"Community colleges existed before Gov. Sanford took office," said one Tar Heel educator, "just as spoke wheels and

Governor Sanford was a frequent visitor at the White House during the administrations of Presidents Kennedy and Johnson.

Industrial Education Centers were expanded greatly to help train the skilled workers so vital in the Space Age.

gasoline engines existed before Henry Ford decided to toss a few parts together."

One thing which has given meaning to the boast, "Good government is a habit in North Carolina," is the willingness of the State's most able citizens to devote their time and energy, often at great personal sacrifice, to public projects such as the school system. Gov. Sanford was especially appreciative of this characteristic, and capitalized upon it.

While he was launching some bold new educational programs, the State Board of Education, the State Board of Higher Education, and various special boards and commissions were taking critical looks at existing programs with a view toward improving them. As Sanford said repeatedly, educational advance results from teamwork.

The 1963 General Assembly, at Gov. Sanford's request, adopted enabling legislation for the creation of some educational innovations that are believed to be without precedent. These experiments have drawn national attention and acclaim, and some of them are being copied by other states. Sanford believed that traditional methods alone were inadequate for a state that ranks 48th among the 50 states in the percentage of adults who are high school graduates, fifth from the bottom in the percentage of men rejected by the armed forces for illiteracy, and around 40th in government financial support for the schools.

Even while some of these innovations were aborning, "The National Observer" was moved to comment: "North Carolina's program to upgrade its schools makes it perhaps the most exciting state educationally in the nation. What North Carolina is doing could lead the way—and make the job easier—for many another state with similar problems but less initiative."

The first innovation was the "Governor's School," which began operations in Winston-Salem in 1963. This is an eight-week summer program that gives 400 of the state's brightest high school juniors and seniors experiences they could not obtain in their own schools. The school is divided into the "gifted," 250 students selected for their academic prowess, and the "talented," 150 chosen for their artistic ability. There are no grades, no credits.

Students who have been able to stretch their minds at the "Governor's School" trot out all of the superlatives as they

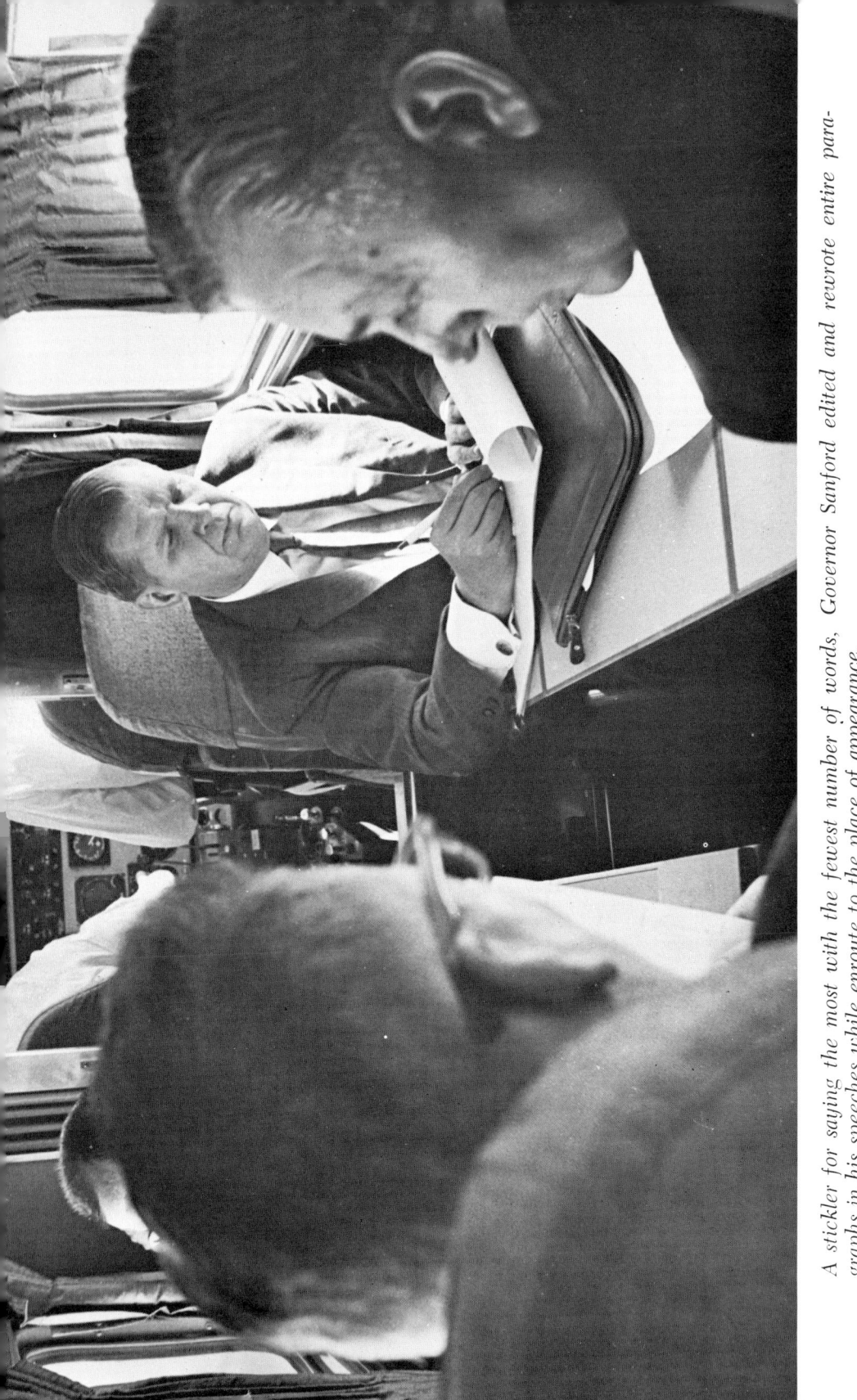

A stickler for saying the most with the fewest number of words, Governor Sanford edited and rewrote entire paragraphs in his speeches while enroute to the place of appearance.

An informed public is an understanding and cooperative public. Governor Sanford worked at the job of getting the programs to the people through all media during interviews, press conferences and breakfasts for many editors, news directors, and reporters.

Governor Sanford talked with students from Yadkinville to Yale and from Harmony to Harvard.

describe the experience. Nor is the school a mere bonus for the bright. Two University of North Carolina psychologists test the youngsters and plan to follow their progress for 10 years. And the school is constantly being evaluated for benefits which may be applicable for the standard high school program.

In establishing the "Governor's School," Sanford fixed a pattern that he generally followed for the other innovations. He demonstrated a marked talent for obtaining financial help from private foundations, which he found were particularly receptive to fresh ideas. The Carnegie Foundation agreed to supply $225,000 to assure the operation of the "Governor's School" for three years, if local interests in Winston-Salem would match the money.

En route to Winston-Salem to unfold the proposition to leading citizens there, Sanford speculated on the length of time it would require to obtain the matching $225,000. The necessary pledges were made in less than 15 minutes.

Sanford's ingenuity in tapping private foundations for funds for the experiments produced several advantages. In the first place, experiments involving only a negligible state investment were more palatable to legislators, who biennially are bombarded with pleas for money. Also, once the experiments had proven their value, they could be presented to future General Assemblies as flourishing projects worthy of whatever state investment might be required.

There were these other innovations:

—The North Carolina School of the Arts, a residential high school and college, which will offer young people standard academic instruction, but will concentrate on training them for professional careers in music, dance and drama.

—The North Carolina Advancement School, which will offer three months of special training for eighth graders whose achievements in school fall below their potential.

—The Learning Institute of North Carolina (LINC), the coordinator of the experiments that will evaluate the projects, borrowing the best from them for adaptation in schools throughout the state.

The measure creating the School of the Arts carried an appropriation of $325,000 for the biennium (foundations supplied

Governor Sanford campaigned long and hard for the Democratic Party. Here he is shown *with* Vice-President Lyndon Johnson at the Jefferson-Jackson D a y Dinner in March of 1963.

$1.5 million, to be matched over a period of five years by private interests). Though it was adopted by a sizable margin, the measure invited wisecracks. One legislator arose and said, "Do you think I could go back home and tell my people that I voted to spend $325,000 of their tax money so some guy in a bikini can get on the stage and do a toe dance?"

His colleagues laughed—then voted aye.

While seeking a site for the school, an advisory board heard citizens from Winston-Salem, Greensboro, Hillsboro, Durham and Raleigh make a pitch for the facility. Winston-Salem landed it by offering free the Gray High School plant, plus $1 million for dormitory construction. Vittorio Giannini, the composer, left the faculty of Juilliard School of Music in New York to become director to the school, scheduled to open its doors in 1965. "It is something I have dreamed of for years," he said of the school that will be the closest thing in the United States to Europe's famed conservatory schools.

An estimated 400 elementary, high school and college students are expected to enroll in the school the first year. Perhaps half of them will come from North Carolina, most of the others from the South. They will be chosen on the basis of their skill in instrumental music, singing, dancing, drama, or other arts and their desire for a career in one of these fields. The students will spend half of their time on academic subjects, half in professional training. The faculty will be composed of professional performers whose schedules will be arranged so that they can continue to perform.

Winston-Salem also obtained the Advancement School, opened in the fall of 1964, by leasing some hospital facilities—six buildings on 10 acres of land—to the school for $1 a year. Once again, Sanford prevailed upon the Carnegie Foundation to contribute, $500,000 in this instance. The U. S. Department of Health, Education and Welfare made a grant of more than $1.4 million.

The initial students were eighth graders, 350 of them to be drawn from all over the State for each three-month session, or 1,400 each year. Room, board and tuition will be free. So the students will not get too homesick during their three months away from home, they will attend in groups of seven from a school. At the same time, one teacher from their school will

The North Carolina School of the Arts: Although it was ridiculed by some as a "Toe Dance School," the Sanford Administration paved the way for passage of an appropriation in the 1963 General Assembly (which was matched by private contributions from Winston-Salem citizens) to establish a school for artistically gifted children.

"First we'll try to get his attention!"

"Beat it, Rocky, this is no place for politics . . ."

The years of the Confederate Centennial saw the Sanfords participating in many memorials on behalf of the State that was "First at Manassas, farthest at Gettysburg, and last at Appomattox."

"It's all yours, Jack, ole buddy . . ."

accompany each group so that 200 teachers every year will study new ways to increase the learning potential of their students.

In announcing the creation of the Learning Institute of North Carolina (LINC) to serve as a central school research center, Gov. Sanford said, "We all recognize that no industry with a budget of more than $500,000,000, which is what North Carolina puts into the public schools during a biennium, would try to get along without a sizable research and development program. We all also should know that a school system in which half the children never graduate from high school is not yet out of the woods. We have a lot to learn."

LINC is directed by Harold Howe II, former superintendent of schools in Scarsdale, N. Y., and is housed in the mansion house at Quail Roost Farm (state-owned) near Durham. Directors include the presidents of Duke University and the University of North Carolina, as well as Gov. Sanford.

"The children who need help are ours, the need is here and is everywhere apparent, and the means now are at hand," said Gov. Sanford. "We have the will, too, a zeal to work together and to begin now an orderly march against the forces of ignorance and poverty which, in this most promised land, are a state and regional and national disgrace, just as they are a state and regional and national challenge."

> *Today in America this goal means that every child should have the room and place to grow and live, to get the most out of life, to give the most back to his generation no matter where born, no matter who his parents or how much money they might have or might not have, no matter what his color, no matter what the extent of his capacity or the limitations of his abilities.*

During Gov. Sanford's administration, "The National Observer" said, "It has gotten to the point where announcements

The Learning Institute of North Carolina, supported by both private and public funds, was incorporated by Governor Sanford and other educational leaders to do research into one of the major enterprises of North Carolina and the nation —education.

of financial grants or new education projects, which would be hailed as major achievements in most states, are accepted as a matter of course in North Carolina. For example:

—"Paid through private funds, a company of New York actors toured the state's public schools for two months in 1963, doing scenes from Shakespeare's plays in period costumes and sets. Many of the children not only had not seen Shakespeare, they had never seen a play.

—"Also with private support, the Vagabond Players of Flat Rock honored a favorite son by touring the schools in 'The World of Carl Sandburg.'

—"A North Carolina Film Board was endowed with $300,000 to make documentary films about the State for use in the schools and elsewhere. These are not to be confused with tourist films.

—"A four-station statewide educational television network is expected to be ready for operation by next year. It is later to be expanded to 11 stations."

A visit to the campus of any one of the state-supported institutions of higher learning in the closing days of Sanford's term would have produced evidence of the yeasting educational process. New buildings were rising. College catalogs were fatter with new course offerings. Not all the evidence was visible, as illustrated by a comment from Dr. W. H. Plemmons, president of Appalachian State Teachers College in the mountain town of Boone:

"The progress and achievements this institution has enjoyed under the present state administration have resulted in increased confidence in and prestige of the college, as demonstrated by unprecedented growth in alumni interest and support and in requests to the institution from public school systems, clubs, community agencies, and even other institutions of higher education for consulting services and specific types of help."

The limitations of space preclude even a bare-bones recital of the experiences of each of the state institutions during the educational revival. A book of door-stop proportions could be written, for instance, about that Fountainhead of North Carolina learning, the Consolidated University of North Carolina, whose name is synonymous with excellence. So as a microcosm of what has happened in higher education, East Carolina College in Greenville has been chosen arbitrarily.

"Tell me, again, how you showed ol' Terry by beating his bonds back in '61, Pop!"

At the time of Sanford's inauguration, East Carolina occupied a campus of 178 acres, had physical assets in building and grounds worth approximately $18 million and an annual operating budget of slightly more than $4 million. The student body of 4,179 was taught by a faculty of 232 representing 16 instructional departments. In 1960, East Carolina offered 16 degree programs.

By 1964, the college had expanded its campus to 300 acres, the value of the physical plant has risen to $30.7 million, the annual operating budget to nearly $8 million. The faculty, representing four schools, one division and 20 instructional departments, had grown to a force of 349. The student body of more than 6,500 enrolled had a choice of 10 degrees and 27 degree programs.

During the same four years, a School of Art and a School of Music were created and both received the highest accreditation in their respective fields. To authors-in-residence were added a painter, a sculptor and a composer. The college was selected to produce and perform the world premiere of the Carlisle Floyd opera, "The Sojourner and Molly Sinclair." The college's summer theater in its first year of operation in 1964 drew audiences of almost 24,000 for week-long runs of six Broadway musicals.

The Board of Higher Education in 1964 approved the establishment of an Institute for Research in Regional Development at East Carolina. Purpose of the Institute is to collect, correlate, and analyze data concerning Eastern North Carolina. Economists, historians, educators, sociologists, scientists, planners, geographers, political scientists and others will seek the solution of the problems of the Coastal Plain. A secondary contribution will be the feed-back of research techniques, findings and enthusiasm to the students and associates of the college.

In the arts and in athletics East Carolina is moving ahead, proving itself not only a vital force in education but in the entire life of a region.

The job is not finished. What we have really done is to create new and unlimited opportunities.

Governor Sanford conducted a tour for the blind through the Faith 7 display on the Capitol grounds in 1963. Here he watches as Vicki Faucett of near Greensboro reaches out to "see" the space capsule. Vicki was one of many students from the State School for the Blind who visited the vehicle which Astronaut Gordon Cooper flew 22 orbits around the earth.

Those in need of help are not just "cases." These are people. Our people. They need our help. We cannot do the job by sitting down and waiting for them to come to us.

The date was May 8, 1961, the site was Washington. At that time, Appalachian governors met with President Kennedy to discuss the region's plight. Left to right are Sanford of North Carolina, Almond of Virginia, Ellington of Tennessee, Combs of Kentucky; Kennedy; Lawrence of Pennsylvania, Tawes of Maryland, Patterson of Alabama and Barron of West Virginia.

In 1964 Governor Sanford and the Appalachian Governors conferred with President Johnson on the legislative progress of the bill that would provide extensive aid to the mountain counties of Western North Carolina.

Governor Terry Sanford is shown at his desk with proposals to the North Carolina Fund from 66 Tar Heel Counties on projects to help erase poverty.

This is a time of plenty in North Carolina, and we are thankful. There are surpluses and profits and monetary gains. We have never known such prosperity, and we have never enjoyed such leisure, recreation and the pleasures of the good life. Our schools have never been better supported and more effective.

But all is not well amid the pleasures and the plenty and the progress. In North Carolina there remain tens of thousands whose family income is so low that daily subsistence is always in doubt. There are tens of thousands who go to bed hungry, get up hungry, go to school hungry. There are tens of thousands of young people who have no skills and no present likelihood to get a skill. There are tens of thousands who live in houses a blight on the landscape and indecent for humanity . . .

There are tens of thousands whose dreams will die. Some of this poverty is self-imposed and some of it is undeserved. All of it withers the spirit of children who neither imposed it nor deserve it. These are the children of poverty who tomorrow will become the parents of poverty.

We hope to break this cycle of poverty. That is what the North Carolina Fund is about.

—Gov. Sanford, Sept. 12, 1963.

In 1963, Gov. Sanford determined to try to illuminate the dark side of the Carolina moon. With the help of some key aides, especially novelist John Ehle, and private citizens, he established the North Carolina Fund, a many-faceted effort to break the grinding, deadly "cycle of poverty" in the State. So impressed was the Ford Foundation with this imaginative endeavor that it contributed $7 million, the largest amount it has ever granted for a statewide project. Contributions by the

President Lyndon Johnson's anti-poverty legislation is similar to North Carolina's. Governor Sanford was one of those present to see the President sign the bill into law.

"If that thing really works, I'll take fifty."

For his work in securing another chance for school drop-outs, Governor Sanford received the National Education Association Award in May, 1964.

Z. Smith Reynolds and Mary Reynolds Babcock foundations of Winston-Salem, plus state and local funds, gave the new agency a total of $14 million.

The Fund assists and lends financial support to local communities, which must shoulder the burden of identifying the causes of poverty and then developing the means of rooting out those causes. The localities enlist the aid of educational, civic, welfare and public groups for an organized, coordinated assault on their social and economic problems.

While the Fund will supply guidance, and eventually will correlate and evaluate the findings for application in all areas of the State, the war on poverty essentially is a local do-it-yourself project. The emphasis is on local initiative, local work. And again, North Carolina was a trailblazer: this is the first experimental program of this type ever launched on a statewide basis.

The Fund invited interested communities to submit proposals and applications for participation in the unique venture. Leaders in 66 of the state's 100 counties met and discussed ways of giving the more unfortunate among them a better chance. Fifty areas, some containing several counties, submitted detailed plans, based on local research and self-analysis. Seven community projects, involving 13 counties, were selected as pilot projects. These projects represent all geographical areas of the State. They are located in urban as well as rural areas, in industrialized as well as agricultural centers.

Mecklenburg county submitted a successful bid. Fund Director George Esser outlined that county's aims as typical of the approach that will be followed: "They want to see, in experimental neighborhoods, whether the efforts of the school, the welfare case worker, the public health nurse, and other agencies cannot be better coordinated to do a better job of diagnosis and counseling, so that their efforts are directed at the whole family.

"They want to see whether the schools cannot be used as community centers, to help develop local neighborhood leadership, to provide education for the illiterate, to provide vocational education for the parent who has the potential for better jobs. They want to see whether through such efforts an attack cannot be made on the general living environment in the slum neighbor-

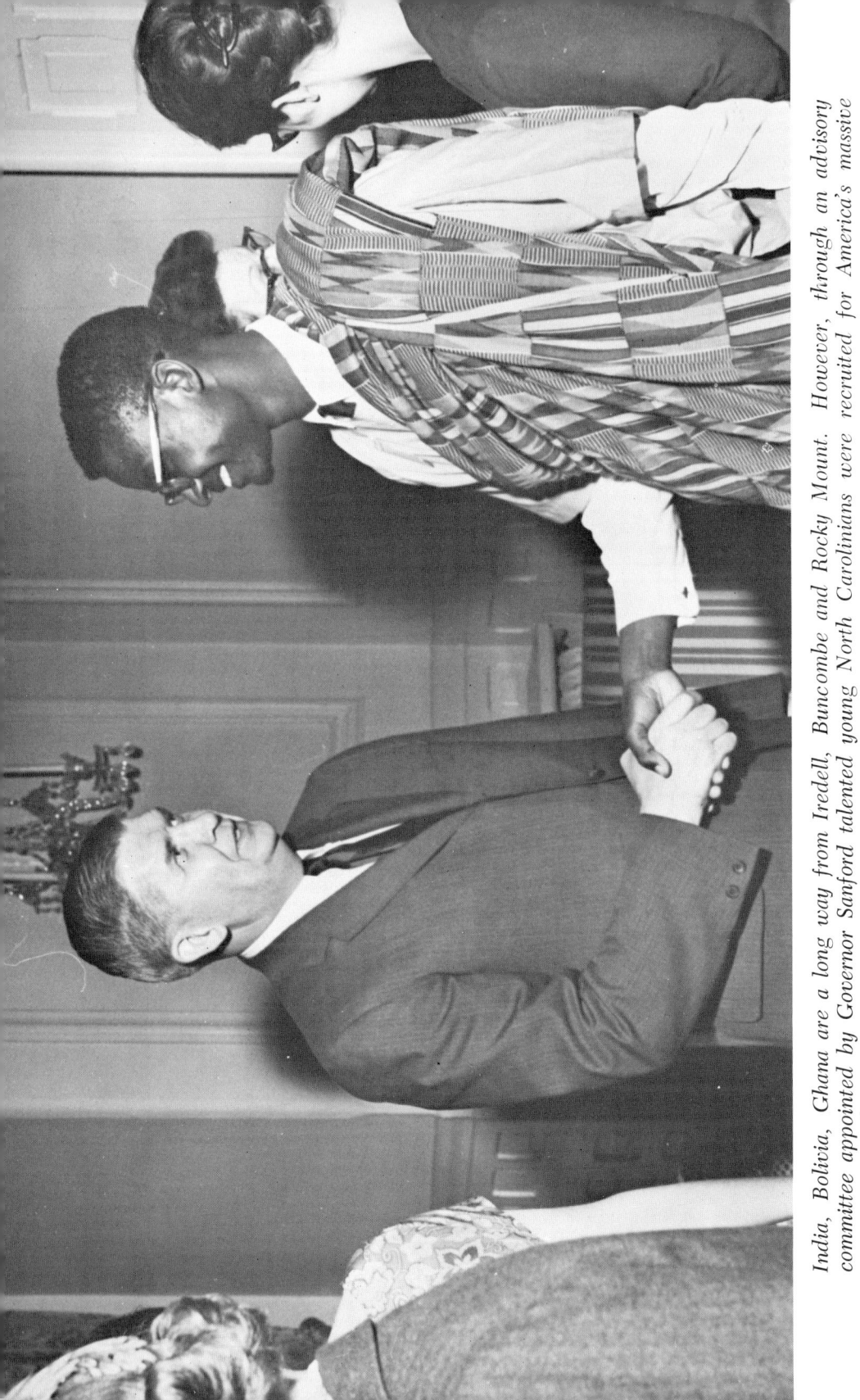

India, Bolivia, Ghana are a long way from Iredell, Buncombe and Rocky Mount. However, through an advisory committee appointed by Governor Sanford talented young North Carolinians were recruited for America's massive peace corps work overseas.

hood, whether housing cannot be improved, and family living habits improved.

"And finally, they want to see whether access to better jobs for the young person and the adult cannot be opened up, whether through experimental programs in the public schools with the cooperation of business and industry or through identification of adults who can be retrained for jobs which are now available without takers."

The first sizable grant made by the Fund was $2 million to the State Board of Education, which the State matched, for a "Three R's Project." This project is designed to improve the reading, writing and arithmetic performances of first, second and third graders all over the State. Research has shown that inadequate learning in these basic subjects in the first three grades is one of the main reasons for the high drop-out rate. The lessons learned here also will be used for the benefit of the entire school system.

Director Esser and Fund President C. A. McKnight of Charlotte expressed surprise at the local reaction to the Fund's call to action. They also expressed the opinion that those communities which were not chosen for pilot projects will inaugurate anti-poverty programs on their own. For these communities took inventory, and what they found in many instances shocked the citizens. The self-examination indulged in ultimately should have widespread, beneficial results. In too many places, poverty was a familiar part of the landscape, but only after it had been examined closely did the community leaders recognize the extent or depth of it, or fully appreciate the cost— in dollars and in lives—of tolerating it in a humane society. Self-analysis is sometimes painful, they found, but always educational.

Gov. Sanford and Fund officials were gratified when federal officials patterned the local action phase of President Lyndon Johnson's anti-poverty legislation after North Carolina's plan. Johnson, in recognition of the State's pioneering effort, summoned Sanford to Washington as a witness when the President signed the anti-poverty measure.

In the summer of 1964, the Fund sent 100 North Carolina Volunteers—college students from every part of the State—to work in the seven pilot communities. The purpose of the Peace

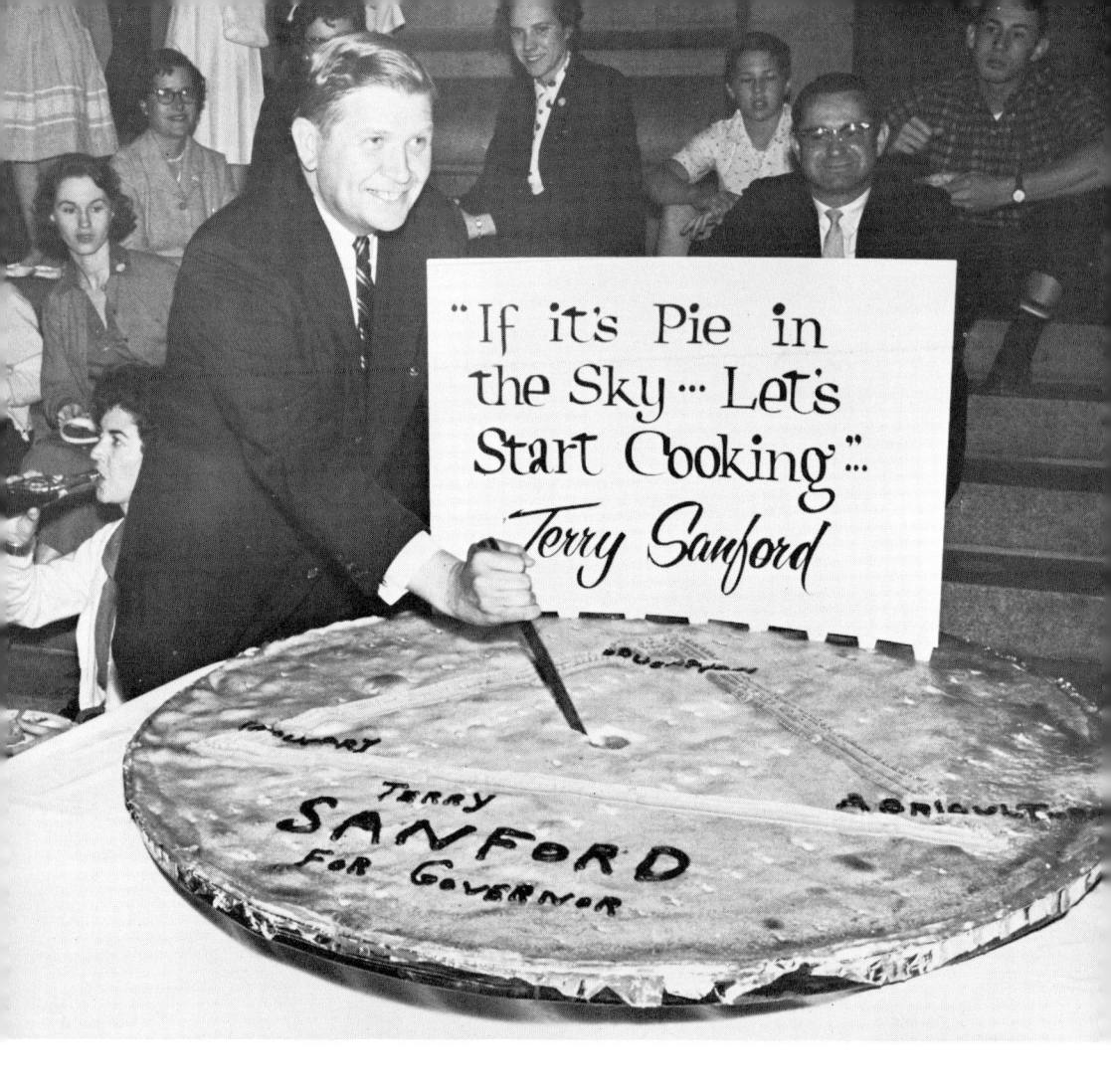

Serious about the business of the State, occasionally Governor Sanford showed a streak of whimsy such as this during his campaign for the Governor's seat. Some of his campaign promises were called "Pie in the Sky." Of all promises made by Candidate Sanford during his bid for the job, Governor Sanford kept 100 per cent, often fulfilling them beyond the original promises.

Corps-style organization was to experiment with ways in which college students can be useful in community actions against poverty.

Announcement of the project produced 750 applications for the 100 positions. Living in the communities in which they worked, the Volunteers received room and board, plus $250 for a summer's work.

Besides pushing organized programs to help the less fortunate, Sanford personally appealed to appropriate state department heads to lend a hand. During the Christmas holidays in 1962, he told them, "I saw a raggedy-clothed boy who had worn his shoes through to the cold December ground. I wondered whose job it is to help him and little fellows like him . . .

"I talked with a little girl who I am sure had not had a decent meal since school was out. Her father had been let out of prison, but he couldn't find a job, and I wondered why we didn't have somebody helping him find a job, and if we didn't have access to help for this child . . .

"Those in need of help are not just 'cases.' These are people. Our people. They need our help. We cannot do the job by sitting down and waiting for them to come to us. Reach out. Find them. Seek them out. Don't miss one."

> *I am not satisfied with being first in the South. I want the title first in the country. Why shouldn't North Carolina strive to lead the Nation?*

When he campaigned for the governorship in 1960, Sanford promised "The most dynamic program of industrial development and expansion this State has ever seen." The record shows that he fulfilled that pledge. Investment in new and expanded plants amounted to more than one billion dollars, an all-time high, by the end of the first three and a half years of the Sanford Administration. No comparable period in the history of North Carolina has approached that figure. A total of 102,826 new jobs were created, and annual payrolls were increased by $346.1 million.

In 1961 Governor Sanford and officials of North Carolina State and the State Extension Service set a goal of $1.6 billion for farm income in North Carolina by 1966.

Associate Editor William D. Snider of the Greensboro Daily News recited statistics compiled by Georgia Tech which showed that North Carolina was the industrial pacesetter of the Southeast. Snider then recounted the numerous projects, educational and otherwise, which Sanford had tirelessly promoted. Wrote Snider:

"All these projects give North Carolina the national image of a state on the move. It is undeniable that such an image serves as a natural drawing card for industrial development. Big executives are impressed by the emerging evidence that North Carolina is vibrant, alert and ready to capitalize on new opportunities. Along with that atmosphere the state's credit rating and fiscal health are excellent. This combination of fiscal conservatism and entrepreneurial daring is attractive and must account, at least in part, for North Carolina's good industrial showing. . .

"The very least that can be deduced from these new industrial statistics, along with other imposing evidence of advancement, particularly in the field of education, is that Gov. Sanford has been a far better governor than many of his own fellow Tar Heels have been prepared to acknowledge. Those who still carp and criticize about dead issues and old grievances should take a new look around the Tar Heel horizon.

"They may not like the source of some of the improvements. But unless they are blind, they will have to admit they are not figments of somebody's imagination."

During the Sanford administration, textiles—the State's largest employer—continued to lead in industrial growth. But sound evidence of healthy diversification is found in the fact that the second fastest-growing industry was chemicals, followed by metal-working, which includes electronics.

Disturbed that North Carolina was shipping food to out-of-state plants, rather than processing it at home, Sanford placed great stress on the food business. It paid off. With six months left in his term, Sanford could take satisfaction from statistics that showed 48 new food processing plants, 151 plant expansions, representing an investment of $37.3 million, 2,830 new jobs and an additional payroll of $9 million a year.

In another area, Sanford supported an increase in the State's minimum wage from 75 cents to $1 per hour. The 1963 General

Governor Sanford worked with farm organizations and encouraged diversification. Here he previews a copy of the History of the Grange with the Grange's officials.

Assembly compromised on an increase to 85 cents. In 1961, the law was broadened to cover an additional 20,000 workers.

The Governor also helped secure adoption of legislation to improve the lot of migrant laborers, who annually move into the State to help harvest vegetables.

> *There are signs that we in the South at last are taking hold of our own shirt fronts, shaking ourselves, and are saying to ourselves as Southerners: "Listen, don't you know you have to live in the world you're born to?"*

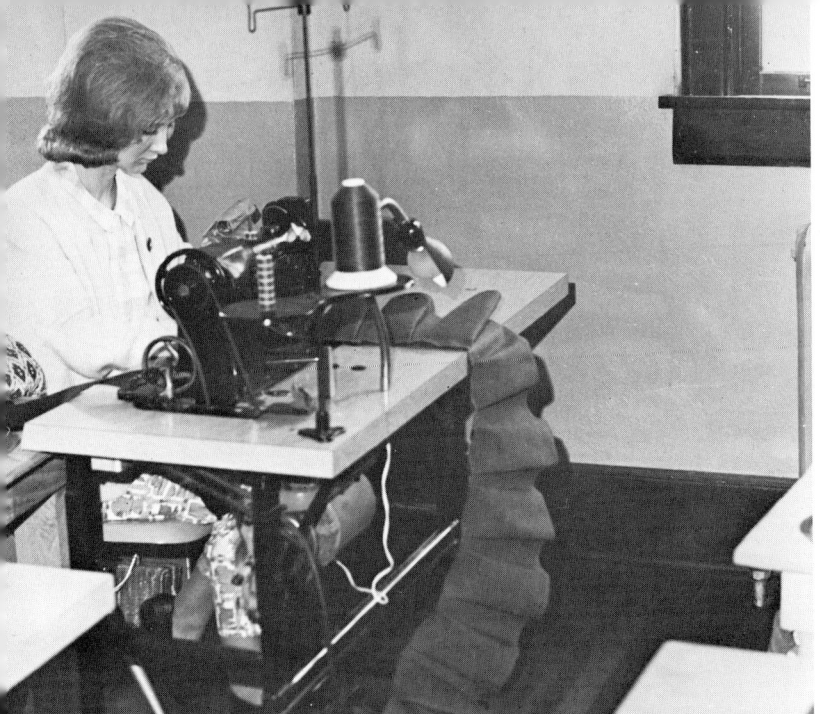

Operation Second Chance put hundreds of young citizens in line for better jobs and an education. During the administration it measurably cut the roll of underemployed and gave another chance to those who needed it.

30 ▮▮▮▮ Drive
Asheville, N. C.

Dear Governor Sanford,

I just thought I would take the time to tell you that I think you have done a marvelous job as governor. I was a dropout until I got to thinking about a speech you made a year or two ago at Crossnore School Inc. Thank you for saving my future.

Most Sincerely,
Jimmy ▮▮▮ Jr.

Interested in all phases of mental health, Governor Sanford reminded the State of its "Forgotten Children" — the mentally retarded — and of the mentally ill. Here he is shown participating in a briefing prior to appearing on television to discuss the South's Mental Health Problems. The show was taped and the tape shown on stations throughout the 16-state region served by the Southern Regional Education Board.

Of all the inventions down through the centuries, of all the discoveries since the time of Eden, of all the miracles of nature, there is none that approaches the magnificence, the intricacies, or the potentials of the human mind.

It is an indictment of our society and the society of other nations that while learning to open canned foods electrically; to broadcast voices and pictures electronically; to manufacture cars with automatic gears and power steering and power brakes and without cranks; to dam the greatest of our rivers; to irrigate the most arid of our lands; to travel safely under the polar cap; to fire missiles across oceans and continents; and to reach toward the stars themselves—that while doing all these things, we have failed to find the solution to the problems of mental retardation.

Address in West Virginia, 1963

In mid-1961, Gov Sanford appointed a special commission to study the needs of the mentally retarded. There are approximately 140,000 mentally retarded North Carolinians, the commission found, and while some of them will need lifelong care, others—with the proper training—can lead happy and productive lives. But the commission found "a critical shortage" of specially-trained teachers who could help train the people with dim minds.

Sanford in 1963 presented his "Proposal on Behalf of the Forgotten Children" to the General Assembly, and virtually the entire program was adopted. The result was that Sanford won appropriations of $44.4 million for the mentally retarded, an increase of 60.5 per cent over the spending for this purpose in the 1957-61 period, and the greatest support ever rendered by a single session of the legislature.

The program included the establishment of a Center for Mental Retardation at Chapel Hill to train medical students and

Many were the foreign dignitaries who visited the State during the administration of Governor Sanford. Here the Shah of Iran, Mohammed Rezi Pahlevi (second from left) watches a fly-by of tactical aircraft, escorted by Governor Sanford and General Paul D. Adams at Pope Air Force Base near Fayetteville, N. C.

residents in the diagnosis and treatment of mental retardation. It included money to train special teachers, specialists and non-specialists for work in institutions and in community centers. Vocational training was expanded, and a special fund was set up to enable the State Board of Health to identify and evaluate retarded persons through a series of clinics spaced around the state.

Gov. Sanford also gave active leadership to the state's mental hospitals. He visited every mental institution after his election and before his inauguration. He supported the creation of the State Mental Health Department, a redefinition of the mental hospital system by the 1963 General Assembly. During his administration, the annual operating budget of the system was increased by $9.6 million. Another $10 million was spent on capital improvements, and employes were put on a 40-hour week.

Typical of this progress is Cherry Hospital in Goldsboro, a mental institution. It got its share of capital improvements, including a building that houses a modern surgical suite with three operating rooms and clinical rooms in other medical specialties. Cherry also demonstrated how benefits radiate beyond the hospital grounds when more money is pumped into an operational budget. For example, Cherry opened a clinic in Wilson, staffed with a psychiatrist, a social worker, a secretary and a nurse to provide after-care for patients released from Cherry Hospital and Dorothea Dix Hospital in Raleigh. "This has been a very rewarding experience and has provided excellent care for the released patients," said Dr. M. M. Vitols, superintendent at Cherry. During Sanford's term, Cherry also added a vocational rehabilitation center that offers training in any industrial field and has been unusually valuable to patients who entered the hospital without any skill at all.

We will reach all of our goals if we give attention to the individual and his chance in life.

Sanford promoted other rehabilitation programs:

—Operation Second Chance: a retraining program in three sections of the State for school dropouts under the Federal Man-

The Work Release plan is making history and saving money for the State. This plan was accelerated under the Sanford administration.

power Development and Training Act and the Area Redevelopment Act.

—Prisons, probation and parole: thanks to enlightened programs such as work release, which now permits nearly 1,000 prisoners to work at their jobs by day and spend nights and weekends in prison, North Carolina's prison population is declining while that of most other states is increasing. Work-release prisoners pay the state for their bed-and-board, support their families (keeping them off welfare rolls), and leave the program with a nest egg.

Sanford extended the use of probation. He dipped into the contingency and emergency fund in 1962 for enough money to permit the Probation Commission to hire 10 additional probation officers. The 1963 General Assembly appropriated funds to add 61 more officers and supporting clerical personnel. When he assumed office, there were more than 12,000 prisoners and fewer than 6,000 probationers. At the end of his term there were more taxpaying and self-supporting probationers in the State than there were prisoners (it costs the State $1,300 per year to keep an inmate).

Major changes were made in the paroles department during the administration. The number of parole officers was increased, and this meant improved supervision for a greater number of parolees. An inmate is eligible for parole after serving one-fourth of his sentence. Formerly, the Board of Paroles began its investigation for parole at the time the inmate had completed one-fourth of his sentence. The board began its investigation two months earlier, so the inmate could be released on the day he was eligible. Board Chairman N. F. Ransdell estimated the State saves as a result more than $400,000 a year because the inmate is released two months earlier and his family leaves the welfare list. The board also employed one man whose principal duty is to classify inmates according to their skills to improve employment opportunities. This is believed to be the first program of its type in the United States.

Many State employees worked long, tedious hours. Under the Sanford administration a forty-hour week was put into service alleviating what had been a disturbing and discouraging condition.

> *A man in my office not long ago wanted a little piece of secondary road paved and I explained to him that we had the best road system in the country, that we had as many paved roads as California, but California had twice as many unpaved roads. I explained to him that Kerr Scott had paved more roads in his administration than had ever been paved in the whole state of Texas. And I explained to him that I'd paved more roads without a bond issue than had ever been paved in Louisiana and a number of other states.*
>
> *And I asked him what he thought about that. And he said, "Well I'll tell you what I think about it. I don't live in Texas or California."*

Between the time Gov. Sanford took office in January, 1961, and Sept. 1, 1964, the State Highway Commission appointed by him had built more secondary roads than in any period since Gov. Kerr Scott's road bond program. More than 3,000 miles of secondary roads were paved, another 5,500 miles of secondary roads were stabilized. The commission paved and improved 1,650 miles of primary roads, opened 185 miles of new interstate highways (70 miles are under construction).

Sanford was able to tell the N. C. Association of County Commissioners in mid-1964 that, "We have paved more primary and interstate roads in the last three and one-half years than have ever been paved in any administration. In fact we have paved more secondary roads in just the last three and one-half years than have ever been paved in Louisiana, Maine, Montana, Nevada, New Mexico, North Dakota or several other states. South Carolina, Tennessee and Georgia have from 16 to 30 per cent of their secondary roads paved. North Carolina has just about 50 per cent of our secondary roads paved. In fact in terms of mileage and percentage paved we rank behind only Ohio and New York, and if you use the number of automobiles as a measuring factor we rank above them."

This highway record was made without any tax increase. Most highway fund diversions were halted and inactive surpluses were used instead.

More Tar Heel highways were built during the Sanford Administration than in any other similar period in the history of the State.

Governor Sanford has a stock answer for the question, "What was your greatest disappointment as Governor?" It was the failure to reduce traffic accidents and traffic deaths. It should be added that the failure was not due to gubernatorial unconcern or inactivity. Even before he took office, he dispatched two people to the National Safety Council in Chicago for suggestions as to what the state could do to cut down the highway carnage.

Sanford followed every suggestion. He made safety legislation the subject of a special message to the General Assembly. He set up the N. C. Traffic Safety Council with private funds. He established a coordinating committee between the Department of Motor Vehicles and the State Highway Commission. He has in operation a special commission that is working on an entirely new concept of traffic law enforcement.

The 1963 General Assembly responded to Sanford's plea for action to such an extent that he was able to say after the session that the legislature adopted the strongest safety legislation "that has been adopted by any one session of the General Assembly since the T-Model started riding the roads in the State." That legislation legalized chemical tests for drunken driving suspects, and tightened instruction in driver education, among other things.

But despite all this, traffic accidents and deaths have continued to increase. As Gov. Sanford said. "that is the ultimate test." Hence his disappointment and sorrow.

The Governor is hopeful that implementation of the new judicial article in the State Constitution, perhaps incorporating special traffic courts, will have a beneficial effect on the traffic toll.

Sanford took to the stump on behalf of court improvements before he was elected Governor, induced the 1961 General Assembly to submit the constitutional amendment to the people, and gave full support to the 1962 campaign that culminated in its adoption by an overwhelming margin.

The following capsule summaries of other areas of activity show not only the progress made during the 1960-64 period, but also the range and diversity of State activities over which a governor presides:

State Ports: Business at the State Ports almost doubled during the Sanford Administration.

For Juveniles

The Board of Juvenile Correction employed for the first time a director of education to supervise the instructional program in all of the correction and training schools, and a farm director to supervise farm operations which provide occupational therapy for the young people and good food for the schools. A juvenile evaluation center was established at Swannanoa in the old Moore General Hospital to treat juveniles with severe emotional problems and behavior difficulties. Sanford named the Governor's Committee on Juvenile Delinquency and Youth Crime to try and prevent delinquency.

For the Deaf

The Eastern North Carolina School for the Deaf was created in Wilson. An estimated $500,000 was saved by using State land and two buildings that were part of the Eastern N. C. Sanatorium for the site. The 1963 General Assembly appropriated $980,000 for construction and equipment for the first phase of the school. The existing school for the deaf in Morganton received money to establish new vocational courses, to build a gymnasium, and to increase teacher pay.

For the Blind

The Commission inaugurated glaucoma screening clinics in which 50,894 people were screened to detect the possible presence of glaucoma (second only to cataracts in the cause of blindness). This program attracted national attention and led to a federally-sponsored research program. During the four-year period, the commission led the nation in the number of visually impaired people rehabilitated into employment.

For State Ports

State Ports Authority revenues increased from $3 million to $5 million. A $16.5 million construction program was launched at Morehead City and Wilmington. Tonnage set new records.

For Medical Care

The volume of construction for hospitals and other medical facilities was much greater than for any four-year period in history. Seven new hospitals were programmed along with three

Tar Heel drivers must renew their driving privileges every four years, face stiff tests administered by over 200 examiners of the Motor Vehicles Department.

The highway patrol, in emergencies, can take to the air. Two light planes enable troopers to widen their activities in hunting down criminals or unsnarling traffic jams.

Courtesy and service are bywords in the State Highway Patrol. Assistance is cheerfully offered travelers day and night by 650 members of the organization who patrol millions of miles annually.

Speeders are detected electrically along unadvertized sections of Tar Heel highways. Known colloquially as "whammies," electric speed zones are manned by troopers to protect innocent motorists. Violators are promptly arrested.

new public health centers, two schools of nursing, six nursing homes, five rehabilitation facilities and two diagnostic and treatment centers. Total cost of projects: $66.4 million, of which the state supplied 1.4 per cent, local communities 50 per cent and the federal government 48.6 per cent.

State Personnel

The work week was reduced to 40 hours. Workers subject to the State Personnel Act got a five per cent across-the-board pay increase in 1961, and the 1963 General Assembly added another $120 per year across-the-board increase. The plan of automatic merit increments, costing a total of $20 million, equivalent to more than an additional ten per cent in salary increases, was continued. The 1961 and 1963 General Assemblies appropriated $3.5 million for increases in salaries to meet competition. A longevity pay plan was liberalized and retirement benefits greatly increased.

Local Public Health

State appropriations for local health departments (aid to counties) were increased by $790,536, the first increase in State aid since 1949.

Teachers' and State Employees' Retirement

Benefits increased for early and late retirement. Retirement pay for women increased by 15 per cent, to put them on par with men. State contributions to the retirement system rose by $95.1 million during the four-year period.

Utilities

Investor-owned electric companies increased their installed generating capacity from three and a half million to more than five million kilowatts and have other facilities under construction which will add another one million kilowatts. (Electric rates in the State for all classes of service are well below the national average). The 34 investor-owned telephone companies have installed 258,000 new telephones. The seven natural gas utilities have approximately doubled their sales since 1960, from 37 to 68 billion cubic feet.

Electric cooperatives during the period built 7,613 miles of rural power lines serving 149,656 rural consumers and received

Highway Safety: More traffic safety legislation was passed during the Sanford Administration than in any administration since the Model-T Ford made its appearance. The governor also gained private funds for the establishment of the North Carolina Traffic Safety Council.

more than 21 million in loan funds from the Rural Electrification Administration. Telephone cooperatives built nearly 8,000 miles of line, and carried telephone service to more than 40,000 rural subscribers, and received more than $26 million in loans.

Motor Vehicles

Registration of motor vehicles increased by 345,000 for the four-year period, revenue collections from vehicle and driver license by $7.6 million. More highway patrolmen were freed from desk duties. The 1963 General Assembly adopted a law requiring seat belts on all passenger cars manufactured on or after Jan. 1, 1964, and enacted a law requiring all applicants for driver licenses who are under 18 years of age to satisfactorily complete a driver training and safety education course before being granted a license.

Water Resources

The W. Kerr Scott Reservoir on the Yadkin River was completed. Congress approved the New Hope Dam, key to development of the Cape Fear River. Plans for the Neuse River basin and for the Upper French Broad River basin were drawn. Small flood control projects were constructed in several counties. Surveys of other river basins were initiated. The State's stream sanitation program advanced more rapidly during the four-year period than at any time since it began in 1951.

Commerce and Industry

The state sponsored an International Trade Fair in Charlotte in 1961 and 1963. In the latter year, North Carolina became the first state to receive the coveted Kennedy "E" award for its program to develop foreign trade. A special section was established in the Department of Conservation and Development to promote the creation of food processing plants.

Archives and History

The 1963 General Assembly appropriated $3 million for a new Archives and History-State Library building. Records of 33 counties were inventoried and scheduled, 25,000 volumes of local records were microfilmed and nearly 300,000 pages were laminated and rebound.

Water Resources: A 50-year plan for the development of North Carolina's great water resources was projected during this Administration.

Employment Security Commission

During the four-year period, the ratio of unemployment in the State was consistently below the national average, and it held firm or declined despite an increasing number of workers each year. During the first six months of fiscal 1961 jobless workers claimed $46 million in unemployment insurance payments, and for a comparable period in fiscal 1963 they claimed $37 million. The State's unemployment insurance fund continued as one of the most solvent in the nation, and the average employer payroll tax continued to be far below the national average.

The U.S.S. North Carolina was saved from the scrapyard and brought to Wilmington, North Carolina, where it was established as a memorial to North Carolinians and others who fought for this country's four freedoms.

I promise to keep my eyes forward on the hopes and goals of North Carolina. If we work together for the common good, then all things are possible.

Governor and Mrs. Sanford participated in hundreds of dedicatory exercises across the State.

Governor Sanford's first political activity occurred when he was 11 and living in his home town, Laurinburg. The year was 1928 and Democrat Al Smith was running for president against Republican Herbert Hoover. (Many top North Carolina Democrats, it should be said, were running for cover). In a Smith parade, Sanford proudly carried a crudely lettered sign that read, "Me and Ma is for Al." Later he was to win the presidency of the State Young Democratic Clubs in 1949 and a State Senate seat in 1953. In 1954, he managed Kerr Scott's successful campaign for the U. S. Senate.

Sanford, as a practitioner, knew that politics consisted of a series of calculated risks, oftimes even a wild gamble. He took his big gamble in Los Angeles in 1960, after he had been nominated for Governor but before he had been elected, by supporting the presidential candidacy of Sen. John Fitzgerald Kennedy. Gov. Luther Hodges, U. S. Senators Sam J. Ervin, Jr. and B. Everett Jordan, and a large majority of the other members of the state delegation favored Senator Lyndon B. Johnson for the nomination. At that particular time, also, there was a strong tide of anti-Kennedy sentiment among Tar Heel voters at large.

Despite the criticism, much of which was vitriolic and some of which lingers even now, Sanford delivered a handful of votes to Kennedy. More important, he held a press conference in Los Angeles and at a strategic moment publicly declared his support of the Massachussetts Senator. The Kennedys immediately began capitalizing on the break in Southern support, using it in appeals to other Southerners. And John Kennedy never forgot.

Once Kennedy won the nomination, Sanford returned to North Carolina and launched the fall campaign, making Kennedy's cause his own. It was a tough fight. For one thing, the State Democratic party machinery needed to be strengthened and reoriented for such a campaign. Because of the manner in which he achieved the governorship (upon the death of Gov. William B. Umstead), because of his background (a lifetime

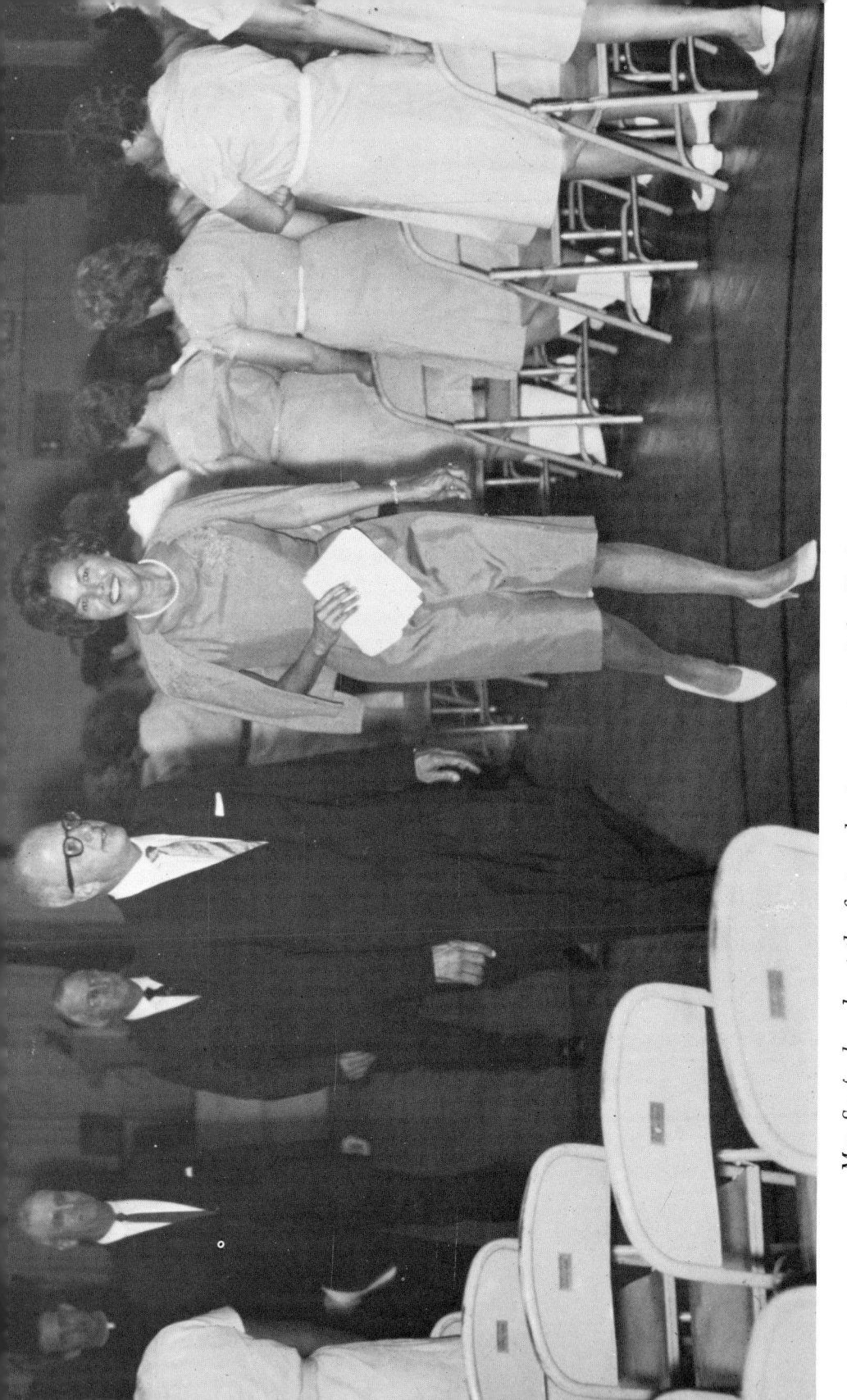

Mrs. Sanford spoke at the first graduation exercises of the N. C. Correctional Center for Women.

in business), and because of his temperament, Governor Hodges had not emphasized party discipline and organization.

Sanford shored up the party strength, and made it clear he and Kennedy were running in tandem. Kennedy would have lost North Carolina if Sanford and his organization (aided by Hodges and a number of other leading Democrats) had not given him their unqualified support. Sanford was still converting North Carolina's trading stamps at the White House when President Kennedy was killed by the bullets in Dallas.

Not long before his death, President Kennedy declared he favored the location of a multimillion dollar environmental health center for the State's Research Triangle. As this is being written, the site of this facility has not been settled. Kennedy's position, however, was indicative of the special position North Carolina occupied in his book.

Kennedy early selected Hodges as U. S. Secretary of Commerce. Sanford tried to secure the post of U. S. Secretary of Agriculture for a Tar Heel, but that was ruled out because it would give a single State two cabinet positions. But Sanford was able to get North Carolinians appointed to the three ranking jobs in Agriculture, a department of vital concern to a primarily agricultural state. A North Carolinian, Henry Hall Wilson of Monroe, was named a Kennedy congressional liaison man, supplying the State with an invaluable entree and daily contact with the White House inner circle. Other lesser appointments also came the State's way from an appreciative President, all of which, in turn, promoted North Carolina progress.

At the State level, the Sanford administration brought women into government. An unprecedented number of them were named to high policy-making boards and commissions. Greater stress was given to their role in party matters, and women finally came into their own as a political force in North Carolina.

The top appointment was that of Superior Court Judge Susie Sharp of Reidsville as the first woman member of the North Carolina Supreme Court.

Sanford also extended greater recognition, in the form of state employment, to Negroes, who comprise one-fourth of the

*Time
for
family*

and a

*time
for
trout*

State's total population. He not only named them to positions at the policy level, he quietly encouraged state agencies to employ them in paid jobs which previously had been closed to them. And to recruit qualified Negroes, he appointed a Negro woman whose job it is to advise Negroes of the new opportunities now available to them.

While comparative analyses have not been made, top officials in the Sanford administration said that the Governor named more Negroes to jobs than all of the previous Tar Heel chief executives in history. They added that he appointed more Negroes during his four-year term than did any other governor in the United States. For the first time since Reconstruction days, a North Carolina Negro—banker John Wheeler of Durham—served as a delegate to the 1964 Democratic National Convention. Another Negro, Clark Brown of Winston-Salem, was an alternate.

All of this helps explain the lack of racial strife in North Carolina during a period of bloodshed and disorder across the nation.

Under the State Constitution, the General Assembly is required to reapportion the House and redistrict the Senate after each 10-year federal census. When Gov. Sanford assumed office, that mandate had been ignored for 20 years. In the 1961 session, the House seats were reapportioned, but the Senate balked at redistricting then and again in the 1963 session. Sanford thereupon called the General Assembly into special session in the fall of 1963 for the purpose of realigning the Senate districts.

In advance of the special session, the Governor personally drafted a redistricting proposal to distribute the 50 seats principally upon the basis of population, at the same time giving weight to considerations of geography and transportation. The proposal was carefully drawn and fully explained. Sanford conducted a series of briefing sessions in all parts of the State for legislators. His basic plan subsequently was adopted within one week. Small-county legislators succeeded in submitting to the voters an alternative plan to assign seats in the General Assembly in the same way seats are assigned in Congress. But in January, 1964, the voters resoundingly defeated the "little federal plan."

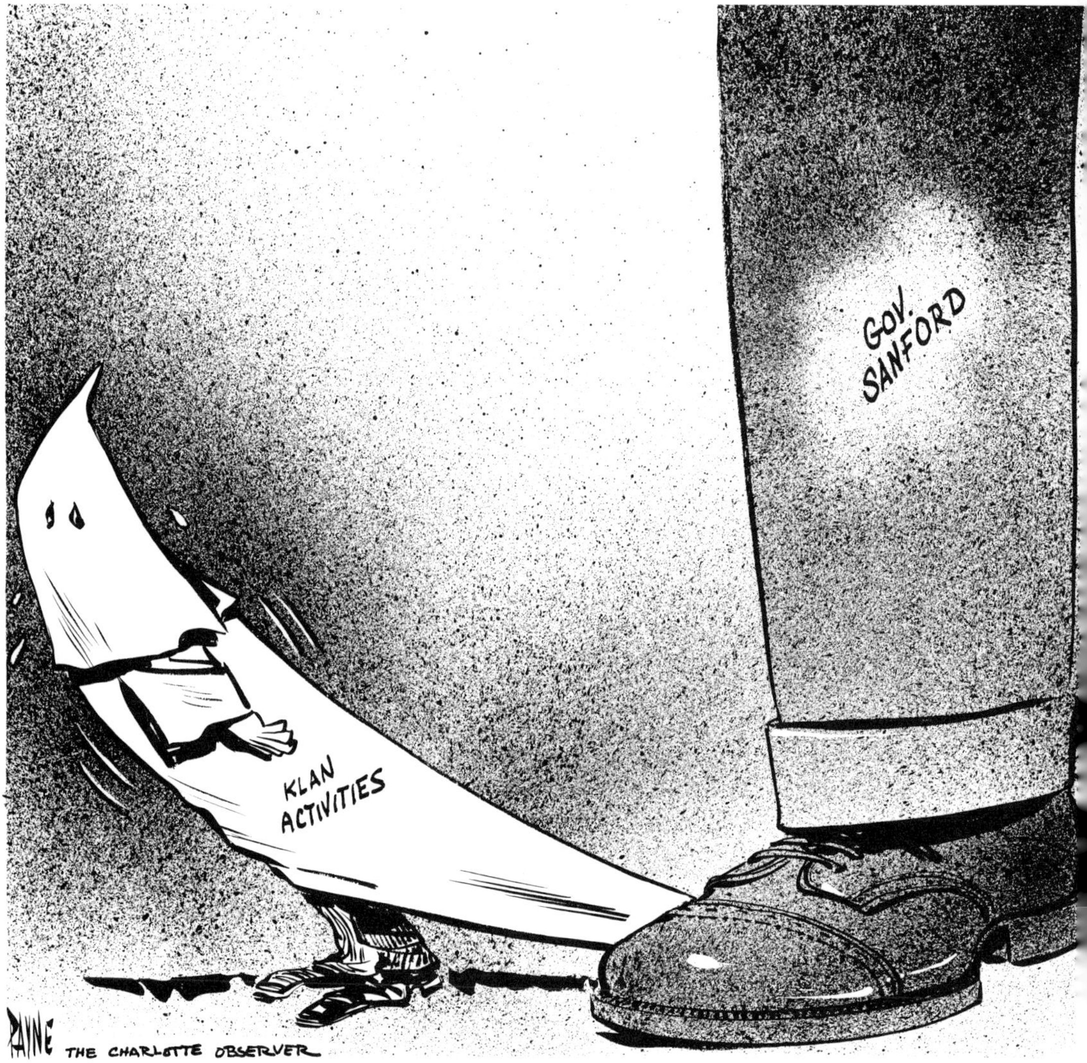

GOV. SANFORD
KLAN ACTIVITIES
PAYNE THE CHARLOTTE OBSERVER

While Sanford was extraordinarily successful in achieving his goals, he also experienced some defeats. A $61.6 million bond issue that was submitted to the people with his approval in 1961 was voted down. The Democratic nominee he favored in the 1964 primaries, L. Richardson Preyer of Greensboro, was defeated by Dan K. Moore of Canton. But as political scorecards go, Sanford fared well, particularly when it is noted that the implementation of his ambitious program necessitated additional taxes in a state that ranks in the lowest national quadrant in per capita income.

On the delicate and potentially explosive topic of civil rights, Governor Sanford adopted a stance of fairness and firmness. He made it quite clear, by deed and word, that North Carolina would obey the law. He said the State would not tolerate violence, from extremists of any stripe. He told the Negro demonstrators their actions had reached the point of diminishing returns. He told the Ku Klux Klan, bluntly and plainly, that the KKK would not supplant law and order. When he felt it necessary, he employed law enforcement officers as a preventive measure. The State escaped the tragic violence which rocked some other states and cities.

Sanford gave more than lip service to the theory that peaceful ways should be found to resolve the difference between men, to ease the emotional tensions, and to find ways and means of erasing the causes of discontent. He had definite ideas about his duty in this respect. "I think leadership in morality is the Governor's prime responsibility," he said. "I think helping develop the kind of climate that will enable local people, local citizens, local officials to work out their own problem is the prime responsibility of the governor. He can set the tone, he can set the example that the rest of the state will be inclined to follow."

Early in 1963, Sanford formed the Good Neighbor Council to promote racial cooperation at the state level while local governments were trying to maintain order and initiate reforms in the face of Negro demonstrations. A fulltime, special assistant, David Coltrane, devoted most of his energies to this type of work. And later in the same year, Sanford named a Mayors' Cooperating Committee whose members pledged to help the

Early in 1963 Governor Sanford formed the Good Neighbor Council to promote racial cooperation at the State level while local governments were trying to maintain order and initiate reforms in the face of Negro demonstrations. From this and the Mayor's Council came a primer for dealing with racial problems: "North Carolina and the Negro," published in 1964.

State and their fellow mayors handle the difficult problem in a way that would safeguard the welfare of all citizens.

The committee of mayors published a book, "North Carolina and the Negro," in which 55 municipalities report their successes and failures along with the methods they employed in dealing with a question that invites few pat answers. The book offers ample evidence that the State of North Carolina generally tried to act in good faith and with good will in a troubled and troublesome area. In a foreword to the book, Gov. Sanford said he hoped the guidelines, explicit and implicit, incorporated in the municipal reports would help encourage continuation of a program based on fair play. He said he was encouraged that not one of the reports "indicates anything less than recognition of the need for action to assure even-handed justice and the full utilization of the Negroes' potential for good citizenship."

For himself, Sanford affirmed his confidence in the philosophy of Gov. Charles B. Aycock, who at the turn of the century took office advocating "universal education." He quoted Aycock: "As a white man, I am afraid of but one thing for my race and that is we shall become afraid to give the Negro a fair chance. The white man in the South can never attain to his fullest growth until he does absolute justice to the Negro race."

Once when he was asked how he felt about the one-term restriction on North Carolina governors, Governor Sanford replied, only half-jokingly, that anyone who served four years in the office would be crazy to seek an additional four years there. Tar Heels who are not in daily contact with the Governor's Office in the west wing of the State Capitol do not realize the exacting demands that are made hourly, day in and day out, upon the chief executive's time, patience, temper, physical stamina, and wisdom.

To each pleader of a special cause, that cause is the most important thing in the world at the moment; to the Governor, it is one of a host of causes which must be fitted into a scheme of priorities for problems affecting more than four and a half million North Carolinians.

An uncommon gift for diplomacy is desirable in a governor; a hide as thick as an elephant's is a necessity, especially in the political seasons.

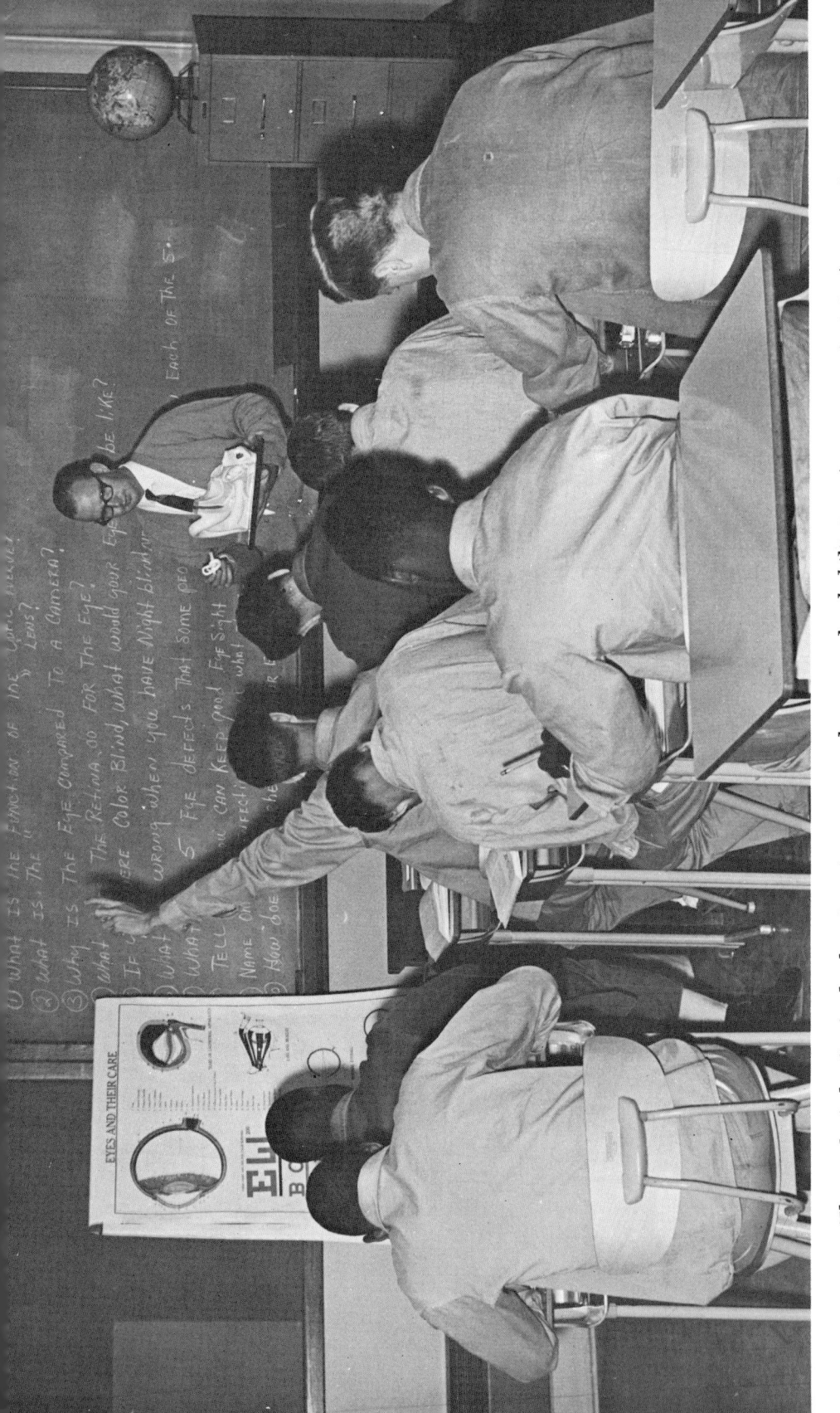

The goal of the Sanford administration was to educate and rehabilitate prisoners—not just to incarcerate them.

During the 1964 gubernatorial primaries, a couple of the candidates began taking potshots at Sanford, who was moved to list some items to which he was giving attention at that particular time (the list changes constantly, always growing more lengthy). Also, the list of accomplishments illustrates that, even without the massive educational strides initiated and promoted by Sanford, his administration would rank with the most progressive administrations in the State's history. The inclusion of the educational program was the crowning achievement of an adminstration whose exploits will, in the opinion of educators and others, grow in public regard with the passage of time, and create for Terry Sanford a special niche alongside that of the first "education governor," Charles Brantley Aycock.

"I notice," Sanford said in a statement on Jan. 26, 1964, "that the candidates are calling names, including mine. I suppose this is natural, but I have something to say about it. I have got at least 88 different irons in the fire, programs and projects and things ranging from special schools for dropouts to seafood research.

"☐ to highway safety ☐ to tobacco research ☐ to inventorying ground water resources ☐ to medical aid for older people ☐ to the development of a phosphate industry ☐ to meeting delegations from other countries ☐ to widening Highway 17 ☐ to school visits ☐ to mountain roads for development ☐ to physical fitness programs.

"☐ to finding loan funds for college students ☐ to the regulation of the possum season ☐ to entertaining industrial prospects ☐ to bridges over the Roanoke ☐ to reviewing requests for commutations and pardons ☐ to arranging for a 40-hour week for employees ☐ to advertising for tourists ☐ to demonstrations ☐ to development of historical sites ☐ to court reform

"☐ to Good Neighbor efforts ☐ to an Appalachian program ☐ to employment of the handicapped ☐ to the reduction of air pollution ☐ to working for community development ☐ to declaring special weeks and days ☐ to extending the use of probation ☐ to the improvement of teacher education ☐ to deciding on more than 80 speaking invitations each week ☐ to prison psychiatric treatment

"☐ to reforestation ☐ to attracting science-based business ☐ to a Southport ferry ☐ to dedications ☐ to rural telephones

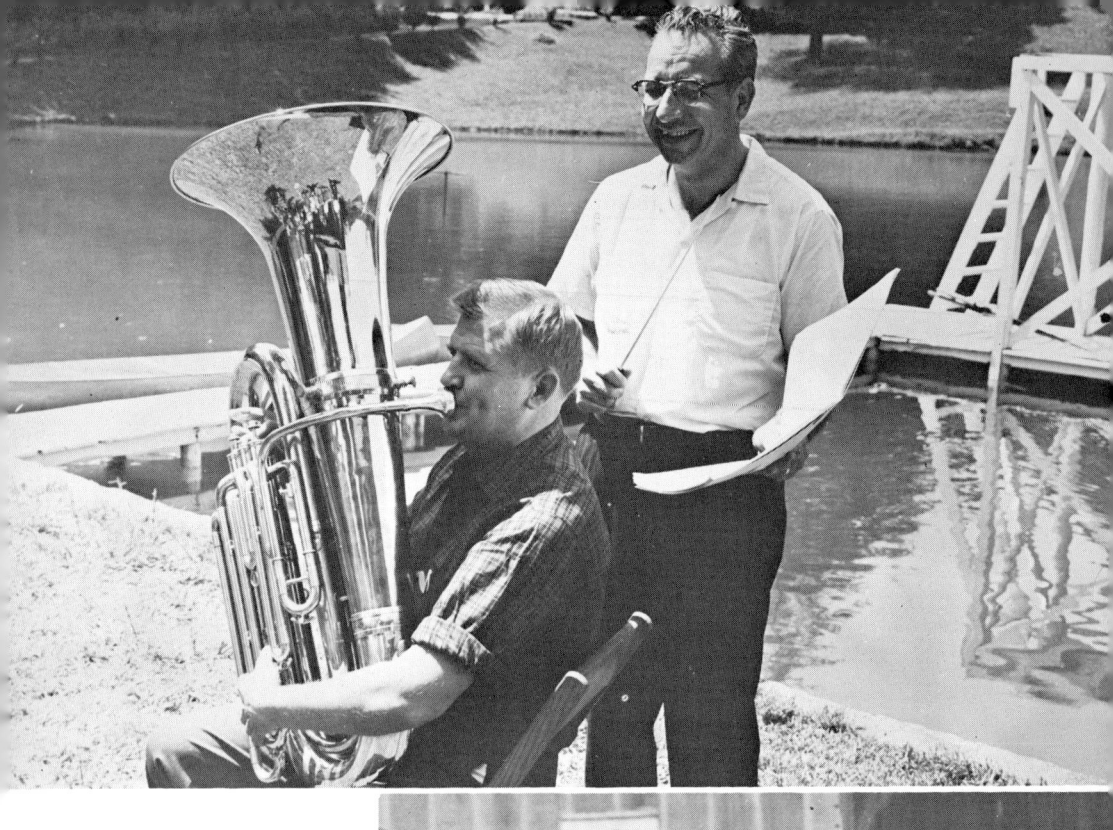

Cooperation . . .
culture to
cattle.

☐ to high dams and medium bridges ☐ to reducing expenses ☐ to civil defense preparations ☐ to community college boards ☐ to helping private colleges

"☐ to getting from Arapahoe to Cherry Point ☐ to education in prisons ☐ to planning for Piedmont Crescent growth ☐ to naming members to several hundred commissions ☐ to increasing exports of farm products ☐ to Heritage Square and Capitol planning ☐ to alcoholic rehabilitation ☐ to helping with sixth grade arithmetic ☐ to answering 300 letters a day ☐ to seeing people with problems

"☐ to presiding over the University trustees ☐ to the surplus food program ☐ to the protection of our textile industry ☐ to worrying about N. C. Symphony funds ☐ to remedial reading programs ☐ to stopping dropouts ☐ to obtaining foundation funds for special projects ☐ to encouraging National Guard and Reserve enlistments ☐ to attracting qualified people to state employment ☐ to maintaining equitable freight rates

"☐ to working with farm organizations ☐ to studying library resources ☐ to working for accelerated public works grants ☐ to improving the status of women ☐ to providing technical assistance for industry ☐ to the preservation of the Outer Banks ☐ to utilization of mineral resources ☐ to cleaning up our rivers and streams ☐ to expediting interstate highway construction ☐ to choosing a band for the World Fair

"☐ to flood control ☐ to expanding opportunities for the retarded child ☐ to honoring outstanding high school students ☐ to promoting the Coastal Historyland Trail ☐ to building secondary roads ☐ to adult illiteracy ☐ to the administration of welfare funds ☐ to development of our ports ☐ to understanding the causes of poverty ☐ to recreation programs

"☐ to children with speech and hearing defects ☐ to promoting the Research Triangle ☐ to expansion of facilities for the mentally ill ☐ to development of adequate industrial education ☐ to extending educational television ☐ to securing the Environmental Health Center ☐ to explaining to dozens and dozens why I left their special interests and mine, off of this list.

"If the candidates will let me attend to these duties, I will gladly leave the campaigning to them."

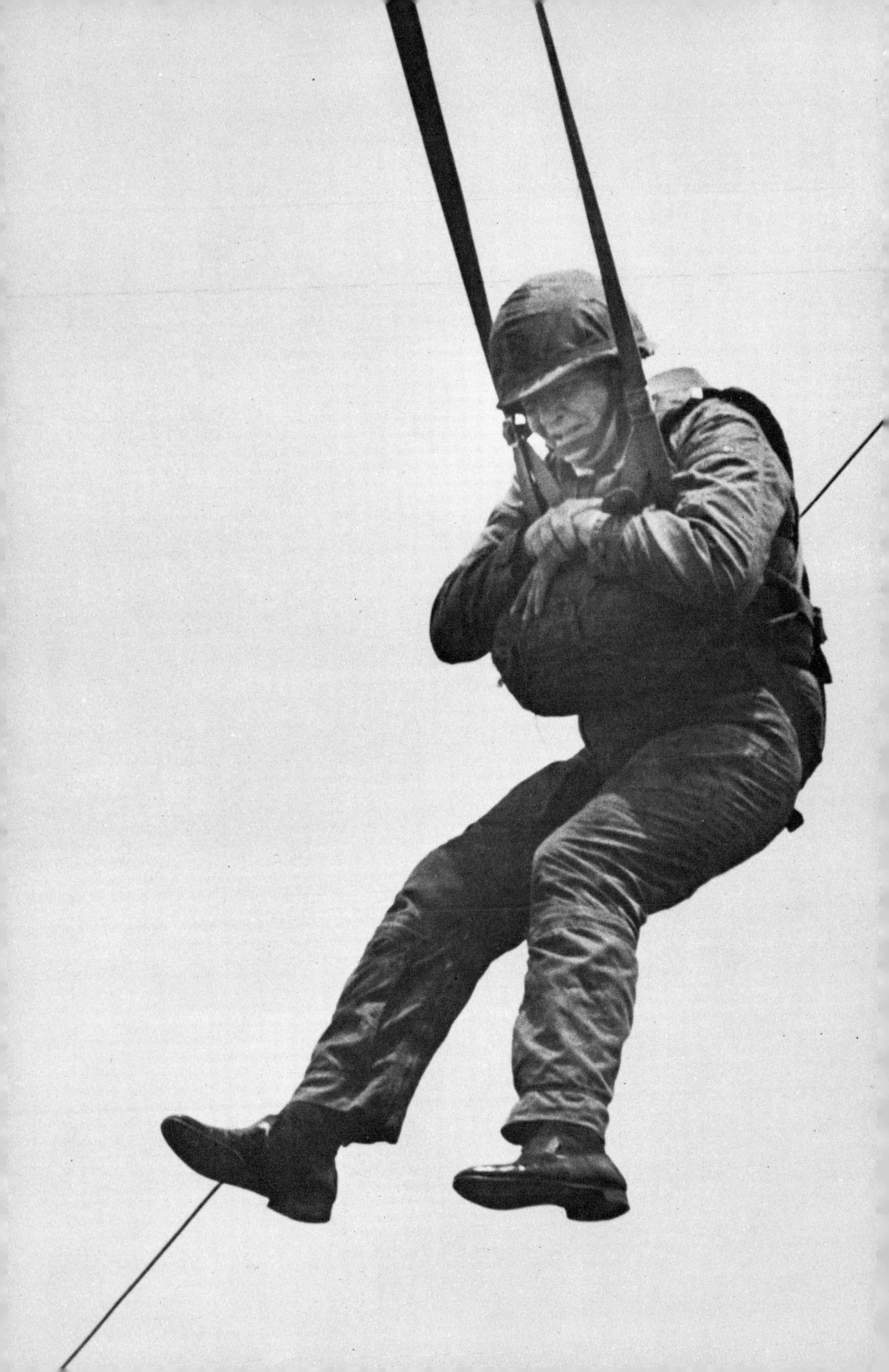

"I'd do it again, yes sir.

And I may."

Home run slugger Roger Maris chats with Little Leager Terry Sanford, Jr.

I do not pretend to take all advice, but I do try to listen and weigh and profit by all advice which comes my way.

—Address in Columbia, S. C., July 18, 1961.

Each Governor brings his own style to the office. Sanford's predecessor, Luther Hodges, was an articulate, impatient type who would scoop up a question at a press conference and run with it.

Sanford always seemed thoroughly relaxed, although the mood was deceptive. An aide once said, "He'd call you in and in five minutes outline a month's work."

At his press conferences, especially the early ones, he was inclined to be cryptic, after the fashion of a wary witness in court, but the relationship with newsmen was almost always warm and friendly. Sanford often showed a penchant for humor. To one lengthy and involved question, for example, he said, "I can't agree with your entire speech."

A sandy-haired, stocky (5-11, 180 pounds) man, Sanford has to watch his weight. He's a golfing neophyte, and enjoys fishing and hunting.

Despite the breakneck pace of his office routine, he was always meticulous about devoting time to his children, Betsy, 15, and Terry, Jr., 12. He and his wife, the vivacious former Margaret Rose Knight of Hopkinsville, Ky., are casually informal and unpretentious. This attitude is shared by their children.

During an exhibition tour in 1961, Roger Maris, of the New York Yankees, stopped by the Governor's Mansion at Sanford's request. The Governor wanted Terry, Jr. to have the thrill of meeting the new home run king. Terry, Jr., at first refused to leave his bedroom. Sanford asked why. "Aw, he tried to break Babe Ruth's record," said Terry, Jr. scornfully.

In times of disaster such as the floods of 1962, Governor Sanford was quick to inspect personally the areas inundated and to secure aid for the farmers.

Sanford once added a new twist to the sometimes grave business of patriotic bragging. To illustrate North Carolina's standing in the textile business, he told an out-of-state audience, "Two out of every four legs you might ogle on any street corner in America are encased in North Carolina hosiery."

Sanford was born in Laurinburg on Aug. 20, 1917, the son of Cecil LeRoy Sanford and Elizabeth Martin Sanford (his mother taught school there for 40 years and is a main reason the son has been preoccupied with education). He attended Laurinburg public schools, Presbyterian Junior College at Maxton and took his bachelor's degree at the University of North Carolina in 1939. World War II interrupted his schooling. He was an officer in a paratrooper outfit that fought in five campaigns in Europe, including the Battle of the Bulge. After the war, he returned to the University in Chapel Hill with the coed he had married in 1942, Margaret Rose Knight, and obtained his law degree.

He established his law office in Fayetteville, and soon had a flourishing practice. He was active in civic affairs and in the Methodist church. He was chairman of the board of trustees that established the Methodist College in Fayetteville.

While Sanford is devout, he didn't parade to church. Many times, on a Sunday he slipped into the back row of some small Methodist church and left as soon as the services ended. On one occasion, a farmer visited the Governor's office and in the course of the conversation Sanford outlined the precautions that had been taken because of a hurricane that was flirting with the coastline. "There's nothing to do but say a little prayer," Sanford said.

The visitor looked up sharply, as if Sanford had offended him by referring so piously to prayer. "Did you really pray?" he asked.

"I did," Sanford said.

"Well, I want you to know I don't appreciate it," said the visitor. "My crops needed the rain."

Sanford has turned aside questions about his political future. He said that, of course, he will maintain his interest in public affairs. Nor does he rule out the possibility that he may again run for governor. His interest in the programs he inaugurated

Escorting...

Speaking...

RALEIGH LPD-1
NEW YORK
NAVAL SHIPYARD
B'KLYN. N.Y.

Christening...

> "As far as Margaret Rose and I are concerned, we've enjoyed every minute of it. We feel a little bit like Miss North Carolina when she said the other day, 'I don't see what you want to select another Miss North Carolina for, anyhow.'"
> —From an interview with Joe Doster and Jay Jenkins of The Charlotte Observer, August 16, 1964.

runs deep. And at 47 he is in the prime of his political career. The only thing he closed the door on was a federal appointment in Washington. That does not appeal to him. Meanwhile, he plans to resume the private practice of law.

He made that plain in a special interview with Joe Doster and Jay Jenkins of The Charlotte Observer on August 16, 1964, when he said:

"I'm certainly not going to Washington to take a job. I don't want to run for any other office right now. I intend to practice law and to take an active interest in political life, particularly in some of the programs that this administration has seen started."

But just as he made plain his personal plans he also made plain his abiding faith in North Carolina and its people.

In that same interview, he had this to say:

"I see for North Carolina an extremely bright future if we continue to put our faith in human resources. Then we will find all the other resources are developed along with it.

"I think the danger for North Carolina is the same danger that America at large has. We will become too complacent and self-satisfied, content to let things stay just as they are because we are doing all right, and we don't need to bother ourselves about other people or other conditions that maybe aren't doing all right.

"Things are so complex and sometimes problems are so difficult that we would rather react in fear and do nothing than to act courageously as has been a tradition of this nation.

"I think there's a danger of that simply because things look so complicated it's easier to say let's just quit altogether.

With two international trade fairs sparked by Governor Sanford, North Carolina told its people and the world about the industrial progress of the State.

"Somehow I believe that North Carolinians are not going to quit altogether. I believe the momentum is good, the direction is proper, and that we are going to keep on moving until in very many ways we will lead this nation in showing how true democracy can develop opportunities for all its people."

That statement contains a great deal of the Sanford philosophy.

A month later, in September, the Governor reflected in more detail on his years in office. In an interview with Staff writer J.A.C. Dunn of The Chapel Hill Weekly, a portrait of Sanford emerges, along with some personal reminiscences of the past four years. From that interview, Dunn wrote:

Almost four years ago Governor Terry Sanford, whose marriage to the State House had not yet been consummated by inauguration, sat in one room of his campaign headquarters suite in the Carolina Hotel. He wore a grey suit and sat very still and talked about the mundane familiar problems of moving a household from Fayetteville to Raleigh.

Last week, Sanford-State House union having long since produced any number of governmental progeny, the Governor sat in his office a few blocks from the Carolina Hotel and talked about being Governor.

He has two curved furrows over his eyes, roughly paralleling his eyebrows. One Gubernatorial term has deepened them. But he still wears the white shirt with the button-down collar and the grey suit, although probably not the same one.

He said that being asked what he had learned while Governor reminded him of "the kid who came home from school and his mother asked him what her darling little boy had learned that day, and he said, 'I learned another kid not to call me mother's darling little boy.'"

Then he sipped from a blue and gold cup of black coffee, lit his pipe, leaned back in his green leather swivel chair (it tilts alarmingly forward and sideways, as well as backward), propped a nattily loafered foot on one of the brass drawer knobs of his desk, and said that what he had learned about North Carolina in four years would fill a book. He didn't start filling it on the spot. He moved on to other Gubernatorial lessons, which, evidently, would not fill a book.

NORTH CAROLIN

"I've learned patience," he said. You would have thought he had acquired this virtue before he started building a political organization several years before he ran for the office.

"I guess I thought I had it, but I didn't really."

He moved on quickly to something else. "Another thing I learned was that the power of this office is greater than I thought it would be. Anything this office supports is reasonably assured of success. If I had taken action sooner on some things, we would have been able to get them done. The highway safety program is one example. It hasn't resulted in saving many lives, which I consider to be the ultimate test. Another example is slum housing in North Carolina, which is something this State should be interested in, and every state should be interested in. If this office had taken action sooner, we might have been able to develop low-cost housing so that it would be a higher standard, with lower or equal rent. Another example is the Crescent Commission. If this office had taken action sooner on that, we would have gotten more done.

(Editor's note: The Crescent 2000 Commission was established by Sanford to promote planning for the orderly growth of the Piedmont Crescent, an arc extending from Raleigh to Charlotte which planners expect to become one of the nation's major centers of population. Sanford's purpose was to prevent helter-skelter growth and eyesores, and to achieve zoning that will make the Crescent as beautiful and as livable as it is prosperous.)

"These are examples of what this office could have done if I had realized the influence the office has, regardless of its occupant, just the name itself carries a lot of weight."

He stopped and relit his pipe. "Ain't that enough?" he said when prodded.

"Well, I learned that criticism doesn't hurt. I said I didn't mind it before the election, but I'm not sure I meant it. Everybody's a little tender. I'm almost completely immune to it now. Before the election it's almost literally true that nobody ever said anything bad about me. I mean, when you're nice to people, talk nice to 'em, you like people, you try to be decent to everybody, nobody has anything bad to say about you. But the amount of bitterness that carried over after the election

At the two International Trade Fairs held during his administration, Governor Sanford participated in helping make each profitable and educational for all Tar Heel citizens.

surprised me. Of course, you're not elected to be a poll-taker, you're elected to provide some leadership. You can't ignore people's opinions, but you've got to weigh them when you make a decision.

"I learned something about the press. It's very easy to miss the point of what this government is trying to do and to get sidetracked into a minor controversy. The press everywhere does this. The press has been very kind to me, but look what happened to the Advanced Learning program. It got buried. But for a week there when the question of colored telephones came up there were news stories, and every secretary was being contacted, and the editorial and cartoon comment was about the colored telephones.

"I've learned to keep my mouth shut. Like when we got that telegram a few days ago about the escaped prisoner up in Swain County, at the beginning of my term I might have had a few hard remarks to make about that, but I just sent the telegram over to the Prison Department, and if anybody asks me, that's all I know. There's no reason why I should know anything about prison policies in Swain County. When the bond issue failed, I said it was my fault. Well, it wasn't my fault, nobody was even giving anybody any blame. But as soon as I said it was my fault, everybody started blaming me. I should have just kept my mouth shut.

"Being Governor didn't do anything for my law. My law's all gone to pieces. I don't think I could even draw a complaint now, and it worries me, because after I leave I'm going to have to go back to practicing law to make a living. It'll be the same practice, mostly corporate law. Not criminal, I started working my way out of that about three or four years before I ran for election.

"I learned that politics is fickle. I suppose I had some idea of that before I got elected, but I think politics is tougher than anybody knows who isn't in it. You've got to fight all the time in politics."

A story is told around Chapel Hill about a gas station owner who filled a gentleman's tank in the early 'fifties, chatted a while with the customer, and later that year received a Christmas card from him. Christmas cards kept coming every year until 1960,

Governor Sanford presides at organizational meeting of the Board of Science and Technology, Camille Dreyfus Lab., Research Park, which he organized to promote the application of the scientific advances of the nation to the industry of North Carolina.

when the station owner suddenly discovered why Terry Sanford had been sending him all those Christmas cards.

"I won't deny it," said Governor Sanford. "That could have happened. I left Carolina in 1948, and I made up my mind to go into public life. When we started building our organization we sent out our share of cards."

He wouldn't say he thought he should have taken a more active part in the recent Democratic Gubernatorial primary. He had an admitted preference for Richardson Preyer, and never took any direct hand in the campaign, not even to the extent of attending strategy meetings, until the last few weeks before the runoff. But he did say, "If somebody's on your horse, you want to have some say about which track he's running on."

"I think that about exhausts the things I've learned," he said, and stepped across the hall to press secretary Graham Jones's office to preside at a little publicity session for North Carolina crabs.

The Governor went back into his own office, where Mrs. Sanford sat waiting in his green leather chair, her legs stretched out under the desk.

The Governor's final comment on the Governorship: "I'd do it again, yes sir. And I may."

The Intern Program was designed by Governor Terry Sanford to attract well-educated and well-qualified young people to careers in State Government.

Governor Sanford established the North Carolina Seashore Commission to protect the State's shoreline and unique Outer Banks from erosion and destruction.

Commission Purpose: To preserve and develop the Tar Heel coastline for future generations.

More than $1 billion was invested in new industries during Governor Sanford's administration.

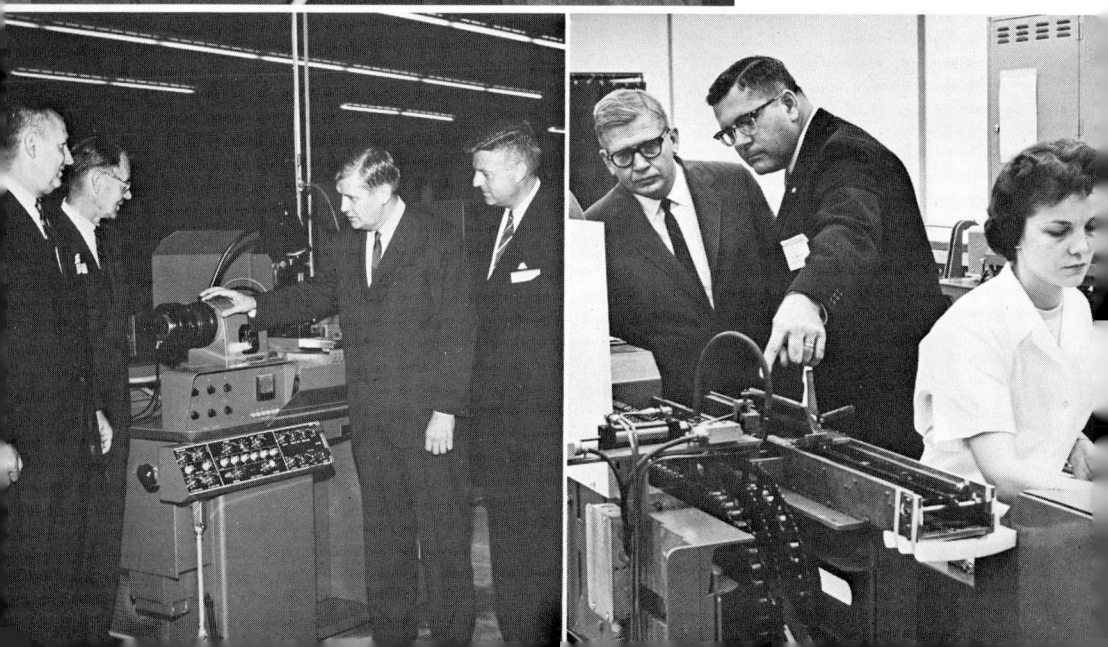

Here he cuts ribbons, both steel and satin, inspects machines in newly opened plants, and examines some of the sea food processed in North Carolina.

Mineral resources of the State were studied and developed. One example is this huge operation of Texas Gulf near Aurora, North Carolina.

Always eager to further cultural advantages for Tar Heels, Governor Sanford lent his support whole-heartedly to the activities of young people. He visited and participated in activities at Brevard Music Camp.

The Governor and Mrs. Sanford personally helped raise funds for the North Carolina Symphony with a Symphony Ball each year. Funds raised by these events helped bring symphonic music to school children across the State.

Court Improvement for the first time since the 19th Century got a shot in the arm during the Sanford Administration when the General Assembly and the people of the State approved a thoroughgoing court improvement amendment to the State Constitution.

President Johnson pauses to address the crowds in Goldsboro on a visit to the State.

Governor and Mrs. Sanford, the youngest First Family in more than half a century, held a 300th birthday party for the State of North Carolina during the State's Tercentenary Celebration in 1963.

Mrs. Rose Kennedy speaks at the Kennedy Memorial Library Rally at Kenan Stadium, Chapel Hill, North Carolina.

*Two sides to the coast...
piscatorial
and
historical...*

THE PIEDMONT CRESCENT

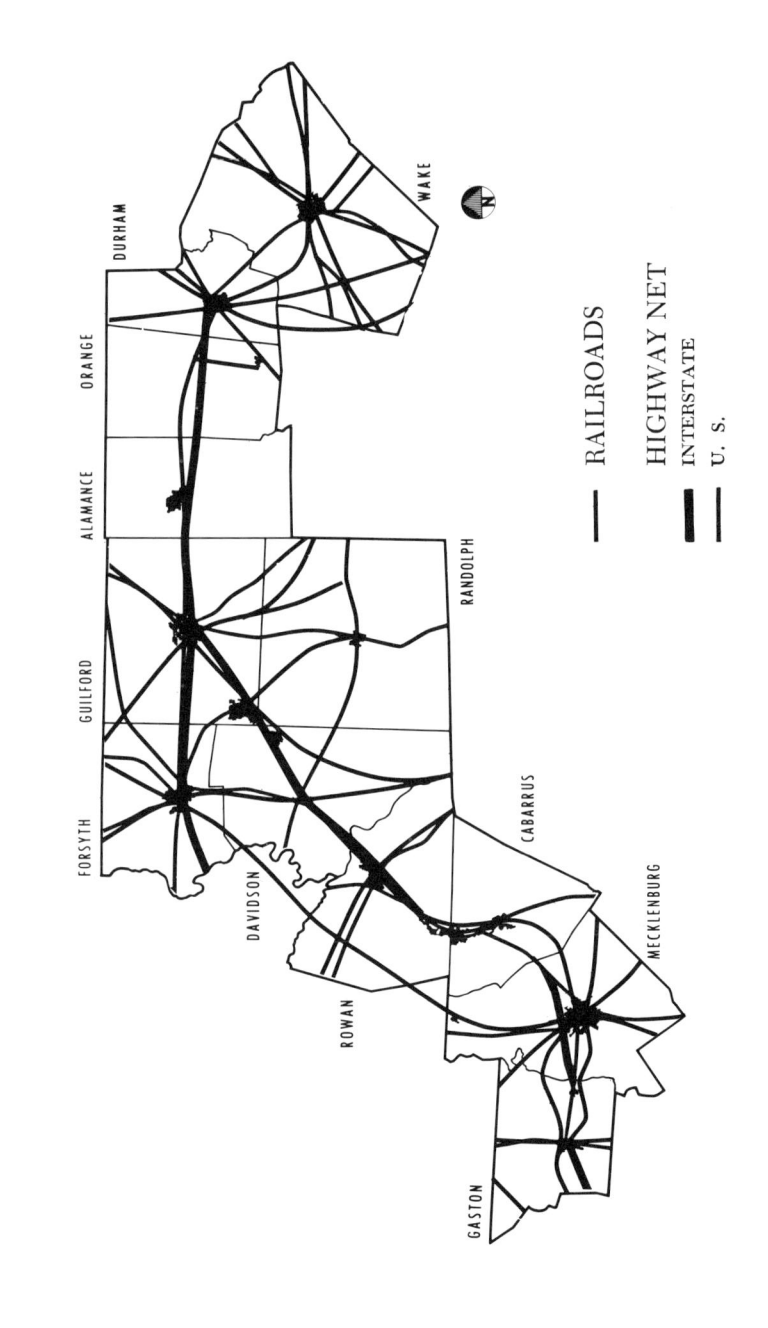

RAILROADS
HIGHWAY NET
INTERSTATE
U. S.

The Crescent 2000 Commission was established by Governor Sanford to tie together in orderly fashion the resources and the opportunities of the Crescent City that runs from Raleigh to Charlotte and beyond. The name of the Commission was chosen because it looks to what the Crescent will be in the year 2000 and because 2000 leaders are working on it.

"What this boat needs is some dam water!"

Selected statements from addresses

of

Governor Terry Sanford

Inauguration Day

We have put education first.—ADDRESS IN WASHINGTON, D. C., APRIL 8, 1963.

It is time to measure . . . It is time to put education first. Education is the foundation of the needs and hopes of the nation. Education, put in the bleakest terms, is survival. And education, put in its brightest terms, is life and growth, and happiness.—ADDRESS IN BALTIMORE, MD., OCT. 17, 1963.

"And now, children, a brand new subject!"

Education is the foundation of democracy. I am concerned with defending the principles of freedom, of individual liberties, of free enterprise, of equality and dignity of man, and therefore I seek the fulfillment of these principles through quality education we offer our boys and girls.—ADDRESS IN CHAPEL HILL, N. C., NOV. 21, 1960.

It is my firm belief that a nation that can afford to send ships under the polar ice and a nation that can afford to grasp for the moon and the stars themselves, and a nation that can enjoy the standard of living that we in America enjoy today can also afford to provide the educational faculties and facilities that the children of this modern age need.—ADDRESS IN COLUMBUS, OHIO, NOV. 12, 1963.

"The Man on the Go — Terry Sanford"

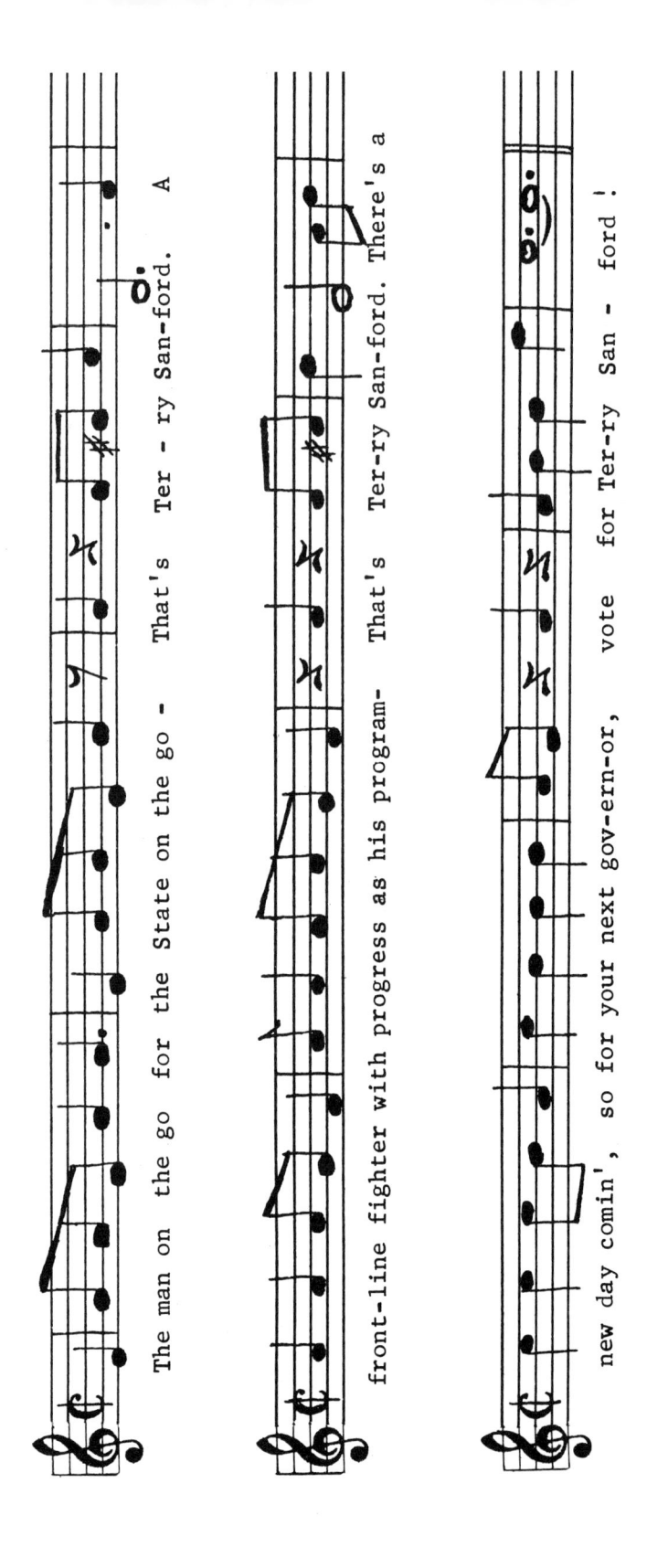

The man on the go for the State on the go - That's Ter-ry San-ford. A front-line fighter with progress as his program - That's Ter-ry San-ford. There's a new day comin', so for your next gov-ern-or, vote for Ter-ry San-ford!

But the hopes of the South, the hopes of the United States and the hopes of our world will rise higher from the desks of the classrooms than from the launching pads at Cape Canaveral.—Address in Hollywood, Fla., Oct. 1, 1962.

I would contend that the greatest force for subversion in this land of ours is not the extremists of the far left or the extremists of the far right.

The greatest force for subversion of our democratic ideals and our human aspirations is ignorance, resulting from drop outs, from those who stayed in but got only shoddy schooling, from the failure of the schools to find a way to encourage every child to make the most of his talents.—Address in Baltimore, Maryland, Oct. 17, 1963.

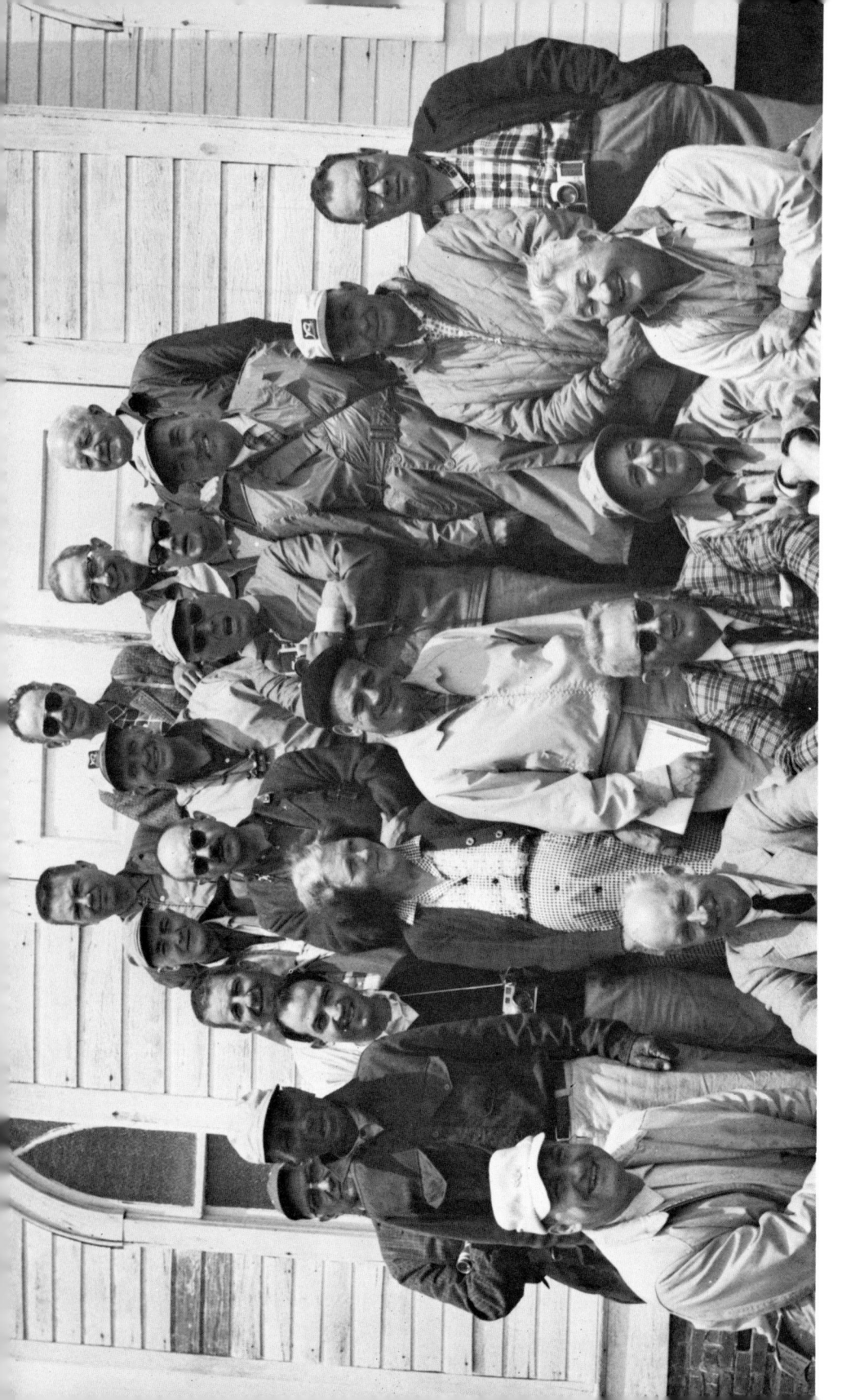

The Honorary Tar Heels held their 1964 spring meeting on the coast.

I'm not so worried about the physical poverty. That is bad enough, but most people can grow out of that. I'm worried about the poverty of the spirit which too often follows physical poverty. Do these children of poverty have the incentives to grow, and learn, and earn, and get something out of life and give something back?—STATEMENT, JANUARY 1, 1963.

We need our own and a new kind of Emancipation Proclamation which will set us free to grow and build, set us free from the drag of poor people, poor schools, from hate, from demagoguery. It has to be a bold dream for the future, realistic in terms of our whole country, and aware that the South is entering upon the mainstream of American life. This kind of proclamation can be written in one word: "Education."—ADDRESS IN DALLAS, TEXAS, NOV. 28, 1962.

What now should be our purposes? What now should be our mission?

We cannot warm over the past and shouldn't. Everything seems so complex now. so big, often so frightening. Small wonder that people look for easy solutions, attempt to find answers in simple alternatives. This may explain the fear so many people have of change, any change. This may explain the rash of organizations and political winners whose creed calls for the return to the "good old days."

It is difficult to see the future, to understand the present needs, to recognize, grasp and follow our mission for the sixties.

Difficulty, however, is no excuse for sitting still, or turning back. This is not the nature of the people of North Carolina, and I am sure it is not the nature of the people of America.—ADDRESS IN WASHINGTON, D. C. APRIL 8, 1963.

Now, a generation later, we can see that our own children are to be a part of a new day too, of still another new day. We can't see its face, can't tell much about it from this distance, can only judge that it will be far different from ours. We can know, however, that our children must prepare themselves to be part of the world, part of the dynamic new South, part of their own new day.—ADDRESS IN DALLAS, TEXAS, NOV. 28, 1962.

Education supports the economy but education must be supported by the economy. As we work for quality in education we must at the same time work just as boldly for broader opportunities to lift the income of our people.

Our goal is not only fully development of the talents of our children, but also the creation of an expanding economy which will give everyone a better chance to make a better living.—INAUGURAL ADDRESS, JANUARY 5, 1961.

DATE DUE